Words, Concepts, Reality

Aristotelian Logic for Teenagers

Thaddeus Kozinski

En Route Books and Media, LLC
St. Louis, MO

Make the time

En Route Books and Media, LLC
5705 Rhodes Avenue
St. Louis, MO 63109

Contact us at contactus@enroutebooksandmedia.com

Cover credit: Thaddeus Kozinski

All rights reserved.

ISBN-13: 978-1-956715-04-0

Library of Congress Control Number: 2021949326

Table of Contents

LESSON 1: *Words*

In this class, we are going to study *words*.

"Wait!" you exclaim, "I've already taken this class! I studied words aplenty in grammar, way back in 4th grade, and way before that in spelling. Why is my education going backwards? I thought this was *logic*!"

Although I think it's pretty certain you have not taken *this* class before, judging by your words, you certainly have some acquaintance with logic. Let me put your words into a formal *logical argument*, what's called a *syllogism*:

If one has studied words, one has taken a logic course.

I have studied words.

I have already taken a logic course.

If **A**, then **B**.

A.

Therefore, **B**.

Your logic is *valid*, meaning that the conclusion, "I have already taken a logic course," follows logically from the two "premises" (premises are sentences in a syllogism that make a claim) above it. But if one of the premises

1

is not true, then the conclusion, though following logically from the premises, may not be true.

Is it true that if one has studied words, one has taken a logic course? I bet you can think of some reasons why it is not necessarily true. Take a moment to think … Have you taken a literature class? Did you study words in that class? Was it a logic class? In fact, can you think of one class you have taken in which words were not studied? Even math class studies words, though they are often symbolic and numerical words, such as + and 3.

Indeed, the study of words is a large part of every discipline, especially those disciplines that make up what's called the *trivium*, Latin for the "three ways," the disciplines of grammar, logic, and rhetoric. The difference between the trivial arts, and, for that matter, all the *liberal arts*, including, among others, literature, history, philosophy, math, and science, is *how* words are studied, to what *end* or for what *purpose*, and from what *perspective*.

Consider this:

Phonetics prescribes how to combine sounds so as to form spoken words correctly.

Spelling prescribes how to combine letters so as to form written words correctly.

Grammar prescribes how to combine words so as to form sentences correctly.

Rhetoric prescribes how to combine sentences into paragraphs and paragraphs into a whole composition having unity, coherence, and the desired emphasis, as well as clarity, force, and beauty.

Logic prescribes how to combine concepts into judgments and judgments into syllogisms and chains of reasoning so as to achieve truth.

You see, it's all words! We could add to this list above, say, history, which uses words to inquire about ... words! ... the words of the past in speeches, documents, and other histories. Or literature, which uses words to convey to the reader an author's experience, whether real or imaginary. Now, of course, our inquiries about history and literature aim at more than words — for we want to know what is *true*, what is *real*, what *is*. The funny thing, though, is that we get to reality through our thoughts about reality, and we think about reality using ... words.

Try to think without using words. Sure, you can imagine something without words, but try to *think* about what you imagine. Think of a bird. Ok, now *think* about the bird: "I like birds. What is a bird? Why can birds fly?" Words! But notice that the words we use somehow involve the thoughts we have, and both the words and the thoughts are themselves like windows for the reality we are talking and thinking about, for the bird itself.

Since thoughts always involve words, we can see how important words are to education, and they are especially important for an education in logic. For, in logic, and especially *material* logic, we study words *as tools of thought*, meaning that we don't so much study that to which the word refers in the real world, but what the word is, and is doing, *in and through our mind*.

For example, consider the word, "woman." I could use *woman* in a sentence like this: "The woman is standing in the room." But I could also use the word *woman* like this: "Woman is a noun." What's the difference? In the second example, I am using the word *woman* as a grammatical term. But in the first example, I am using the word *woman* to refer to a *real* woman, and this is the normal use of words — to get us to know or think about the real world outside our minds.

"Hey, *woman* is a noun!"
"What? Did you just call *that* woman a *noun*?"
"No, the *word woman* is a noun!"
"Oh, good because I think she took it as an insult!"

So, if I say that a woman, or a man, or a cat, or a book, is a noun, or if I say that red, 5ft-tall, or small is an adjective, I am thinking of the word itself, not, therefore, its meaning, not what it refers to in real life. I am, thus, thinking *grammatically* about words.

Now, logic looks at words in a similar way, but not exactly the same way as grammar. Instead of "woman is a noun," logic says, "woman is a *concept*" or "woman is a substance," or "woman is a genus" (we'll define these terms later). Instead of "red is an adjective," logic says, "red is an accident" or "red is a quality." These are not *grammatical* objects (objects that make up a *sentence*) but *logical* objects, objects that make up a *thought*.

Think for yourself...

Answer these:

1) Explain the importance of words in education.
2) Choose a word not already discussed above and define it in two ways: as an object in *reality* (as it refers to the thing itself in the world), and as an object in a sentence (its purely grammatical function).

Ponder these:

3) What are words? Can you come with a definition? When you do, think about it, and see if you can improve on it.
4) Consider what would make a definition a good definition and what would make it a bad one.
5) How do you think words relate to thoughts, and how do both of these relate to the real world?

LESSON 2: *What _is_ Logic?*

Here's a definition of logic for us to think about:

 Logic prescribes how to combine concepts into judgments and judgments into syllogisms and chains of reasoning so as to achieve truth.

We will learn later the meaning of these new words, such as concept and judgment, but even now you might be asking, "But what is the purpose of achieving truth?" Let me go on a little tangent here to answer your excellent question.

There are basically three sorts of "goods" in the world, *good* meaning more than just "I like it," but having real value, not just for me, but for anybody.

One sort of good is something we value only because it can help us obtain another good, and not because it is *good or valuable in itself.* For example, when you touch a hot stove and feel pain, or get a tooth removed, though this is an undesirable experience in itself, we nevertheless choose to undergo it because it enables us to avoid a greater pain, like a serious burn or a gum infection.

 **What is *good?***

Notice here that we value the pain and the trip to the dentist *for the sake of something else that* we value higher than these, in this case, the good of health. So, pain and dentists are *useful* or *instrumental* goods (an instrument can be defined as something we can use to obtain something else).

Health, on the other hand, is more than useful, for we desire it *for its own sake*. None of us would choose most other goods unless we had health first — of what value is the good of a vacation if we're sick? Health is, thus, a *valuable* good, a good *in itself*. Other valuable goods are friendship, virtue, and happiness. Happiness is perhaps the most valuable good, and perhaps the least "useful," in that you would never want happiness for *something else*, but you want all things for the sake of happiness.

Now, some valuable goods are also useful, and some are not. Health, for example, is a good in itself, but it also useful. If we are healthy, we can more easily obtain good things like knowledge and do good things like share time with friends. Enjoyment or pleasure, on the other hand, are really just something we like for their own sake, not for what we can do with them. Enjoyment or pleasure is, thus, useless, but not because they aren't good, but because they literally have no *use* apart from their own good.

So, we have three classes of goods:

> 1. Goods that are only useful and not desirable in themselves.
>   e.g., "It is good I went to the dentist." (Pulling the tooth is the good).
> 2. Goods that are both useful and desirable in themselves.
>   e.g., "I am in good health." (Health is the good).
> 3. Goods that are only desirable in themselves.
>   e.g., "I'm having a good time at the party." (Enjoyment is the good).

Can you think of some more examples of each of these three classes of goods?

So, what does all this have to do with logic? Well, let's go back to our definition of logic. We can see that logic's goal is the achievement of truth. What kind of good is "the achievement of truth"? Doesn't it seem that it is one of those that are both valuable in itself and also for what it can do for us, for its consequences or effects? Why would truth be good in itself? One reason is because knowing the truth about reality is the main purpose of our minds, or, to put it another way, _truth is the perfection of the intellect_. Now, the knowledge of the truth that perfects our minds can also help us to get and do other things we value, such as making good decisions in our lives, fixing a broken tire, and practicing medicine.

The knowledge of logic can help us to think and speak and write clearly and with good reasoning, which is surely useful in countless ways for us in the real world. Nevertheless, the knowledge of logic, insofar as it helps us achieve truth, is good in itself.

The liberal arts — such as grammar, logic, rhetoric, mathematics, literature, history, science, philosophy — are all members of that class of goods that are both valuable in themselves and also for their consequences and effects. Classical education, which comprises all these liberal arts and more, is thus a _good in itself_, even though, of course, it will help us achieve other goods, like making a living, building character, and, ultimately, finding happiness.

What does "good in itself" mean? Is "good" always the same as "what I like or want"? Is something good just because I desire, like, approve, or value it? Or, is something good in itself, and that's why I desire, like, approve, or value it, and that's why I should?

OKAY. BACK TO OUR LOGIC DEFINITION!

Let me translate our above definition of logic into a definition of grammar, and then I think you'll begin to see the connection:

Logic prescribes how to combine concepts into judgments and judgments into syllogisms and chains of reasoning so as to achieve truth.

Grammar prescribes how to combine subjects and predicates into sentences, and sentences into paragraphs, and paragraphs into compositions so as to achieve well-expressed thoughts.

You'll notice both the similarities and differences between the two definitions. Both have elements or smaller parts (subjects and predicates, concepts) that combine to form larger parts (sentences, judgments) to form the whole (compositions, arguments).

Let's unpack this a bit: Remember back in grammar that a subject is the part of the sentence that describes who or what is being talked about or doing something. And the predicate is the part of the sentence that talks about the subject, describing it or what it or he or she is doing.

And when you put the subject and predicate together, you have a complete thought, or what in grammar is called a *sentence*. Every sentence that is a statement consists of three parts:

1. What we are talking about. This is called the *subject* because it is the subject under discussion.
2. What we say about it. This is called the *predicate* (from, Latin for "about" and "say").
3. The *copula*, that is the linking word (*copula* in Latin means a coupling or joining) which is either "is" or "is not" or some form of this.

Concepts in logic are like subjects and predicates in a sentence. And when you put together concepts, you have, not a sentence, but a _judgment_. The difference between a concept and a subject or predicate is not that they are different words or different people, or things, or characteristics, but that they are being _considered_ differently. A concept is just a subject or predicate but is considered, not as a word of phrase on paper or spoken out loud, but as _something in the mind._ And a subject or predicate is just a concept but is considered as _the expression in writing or out loud of what's in the mind._ Huh? An example might help:

> Here is a **sentence**: <u>Mr. Smith is walking.</u>
> The subject is "Mr. Smith." The predicate is "is walking."

> Here is a **_judgment_**: <u>Mr. Smith is walking.</u>
> One concept is expressed by the phrase "Mr. Smith." The other concept is expressed by the phrase "is walking."

Grammar asks the question: Is the sentence a complete sentence? (_Mr. Smith walking_ wouldn't be a complete sentence). Is the grammar correct? (Mr. Smith _are_ walking would be grammatically incorrect.) And grammar is the art that enables the writer to express herself in complete sentences with correct grammar.

A **concept** is just a subject or a predicate but considered, not as a word or phrase written or spoken out loud, but as something in the mind.

Logic, on the other hand, asks the question: Is the sentence possibly a truthful judgment? Is the judgment logically correct?

Consider this sentence and judgment: "Man is a Mr. Smith." Is it grammatically correct? Yes! It's absurd, of course, but does it break any grammar rules? But is it logically correct? We will learn later the precise reason it is not, but for now, I think you can figure it out in your own way.

In grammar, the purpose or end is to achieve *well-expressed thoughts*, while the purpose or end of logic is to achieve *truth*.

Think about this for a few minutes ...

 What's the difference between saying that a sentence is well-expressed and saying that it is true?

Hopefully, you will have made some distinctions, perhaps some version of these:

1) Not all well-expressed thoughts are true: "Man is a Mr. Smith" is well-expressed (it has correct grammar (parts of speech) and syntax (the relation of parts of speech). But it's not true.

2) Badly-expressed thoughts can be true: "People be doing stuff sometimes" is not well expressed (it lacks precision and is a but slangy), but it's true.

Good use of words and sentences and paragraphs is very important, and that's why you spend a lot of time in school and at home practicing the art of grammar. But what is the *purpose* of using words well? You might answer, "To express my thoughts well." Ok, right! But keep going.

What is the purpose of expressing our thoughts well, both to ourselves and to others? We know in our hearts that we should not use our words to say something different than what is in our thoughts, in other words, to lie. Of course, we don't need to say *everything* that is in our thoughts at all times and to everyone we meet. And we most probably shouldn't.

But whatever we *do say*, it should be what we *mean*, meaning that our words should correspond to our thoughts.

Truth is the union of world and mind, thing and thought, reality and soul.

Now, why is that, you suppose? Why should our words correspond with our thoughts? In short, why should we be truthful? Well, this isn't a class on ethics, but on logic, so we can't really get to the bottom of this question here — but feel free to think about it more and discuss it with your friends and family.

The classical understanding (what the ancient Greeks and Roman philosophers, and medieval monks, and American Founders, for example. would have understood) of the purpose of expressing, and expressing as well as we can, our thoughts in words, both to ourselves and to others, is to seek after, attain, and share *truth*. And the reason for *this* is that the purpose of *thought* itself is to be a mirror of truth, of reality, of the way things are.

Truth, in this understanding, is the *identity of thought with things, mind with reality, perception with what is*. When we obtain truth, it's because our thoughts and judgments have become, to some extent, clear and accurate mirrors of reality.

Falsity, to use the mirror metaphor, is when our minds distort reality, like a fun-house mirror. We also want the sentences we write and say to be clear and accurate mirrors of our thoughts, as well as well-expressed. So, in short, we practice grammar, that is, we express our thoughts well in words, for the sake of thinking well, and we want to think well for the sake of knowing and sharing truth. We go back to grammar to express well the truths we have discovered, and then also back to logic to make sure our thoughts and arguments about the truth we have discovered are accurate and valid. It's an endless, beautiful circle!

There are two main divisions of logic: formal logic and material logic. Formal logic has to do with *judgments* (what you learned in grammar as *sentences*) and *syllogisms* (a fancy term for *arguments*), and material logic has to do with *concepts* (what you learned in grammar as *nouns*). So, this year, we will be talking about concepts, *all about* concepts. Next year, some of you will take on judgments and syllogisms, and some of you have already studied these. But before we get to talking about concepts, let's talk about the **big picture** of logic.

Think for yourself...

Answer these:

1) What are the three classes of goods?
2) What is a concept?
3) What are some similarities between grammar and logic? What are some differences?
4) Why is logic more concerned with truth than grammar?

Ponder these:

5) Choose one truth that you know and put it in the form of a sentence. Say it to yourself. What does it *feel* like to know this truth? What do you think is the relation of our feelings to truth?
6) If feeling is one way to know when something is true, and if logic really is *not* about feelings but thoughts, then how can logic help up to know truth?
7) Look back at the definition of truth given in the text. Based on this definition, can you come up with a test that will accurately guarantee when we have discovered the truth about something?

LESSON 3: *The Big Picture*
The Intellect in Three Acts

The paragraph is the smallest version of a "finished product" in the art of writing. The essay and the book are larger versions. Let's focus on the paragraph. One could say that there are three "acts" that go into producing a paragraph. The first act is the selection of good, meaningful, and clear words. The second is putting these words together in grammatically correct sentences. And the third is putting the sentences together into a coherent and orderly paragraph. These three acts have a parallel in logic, in the art and science of thinking.

When we think, we, of course, use words, just like in writing or speaking. But in logic, we are focusing on that to which the word refers in our mind. This we call the *concept*. And so the formation of a concept is the *first act of the mind*. A concept is a mental version of what exists in reality. For example, when we see a black cat walk across our path, we can't help but think of "cat." Obviously, the actual cat is not in our mind — that would hurt! But somehow the cat a few feet from us and the concept "cat" that is now in our minds are identical. It is, after all, the cat next to us that we are thinking *about*. What we *know* is that black cat, and the formation of the concept of *cat* is the act of the mind *by which we know that cat*.

More on how this happens later. The formation of a word that signifies the concept is what enables us to communicate our concepts with each other. That word which clearly signifies one concept is called a *term*.

 The formation of a concept, or the simple apprehension of what something is, is **the first act of the intellect**.

So, the first act of the intellect is the *simple apprehension* of what something is. It's *simple*, because it can be reduced to one thing, namely, the *essence* of something, in this case, the essence of that black furry thing with four legs, namely, a cat. The essence of something is just *what it is*, what *kind of being* it is, what makes it *this* being and not *another* being. So, the essence of that black, meowing, cute, four-legged furry being sauntering across your path is "cat." Simple! It's also simple because you don't do anything in your mind with the thing — you just *know it*. That is, you don't *judge* it. I don't mean here by "judge" a moral judgment like, "That cat is an evil cat," but just any *affirmation* or *denial* using the word "cat" as the subject of a sentence, such as, "The cat is black" or even just, "That is a cat."

 A **concept** is a mental version of what exists in reality.

 A **term** is a verbal version of what exists in reality.

Now, when you saw this cat, you probably didn't just think "cat" but also thought to yourself, made a judgment like, "That's a cat," or "Look at that cat," or "I like (or hate) that cat," or "Someone must have lost their cat." You may even have syllogized to yourself, "Since that cat walked past me, I may have bad luck today!" This is the normal way we think, making judgments — "That's a cat" — and inferences — "Someone must have lost their cat" — and arguments — "Since . . . bad luck!" about the objects we experience through the concepts we form of them.

When we think, in other words, we don't just say to ourselves or others, "cat." That is, we never stop in our thinking with the first act of the intellect, but always move on to the second act, judgment, and the third act, reasoning or argument. In order to stop at the first act, we would need to really stop our thoughts by a great act of the will to stop judging and inferring and arguing. You can try it now for yourself right now.

> **Try to just think of something like a cat, or a tree, or logic, and not make any judgments, inferences, or arguments about it.**

But although we can't in practice not think in "three acts," we can analyze each act in the abstract, and that's what logic does.

Getting back to our phrase, *simple apprehension.* The first act of the intellect is not just simple, but an *apprehension.* This is because you "take hold" (the meaning in Latin of the root word, *apprehendere*) of the thing in the world with your mind by the concept that your mind forms.

> **Simple apprehension:** The act of the intellect by which we form a concept of the essence of something.

We will be spending all our time in this course talking about the first act of the intellect, for this is what *material* logic studies. You will learn about the other two acts in detail in a future logic course, *formal* logic.

Let's talk about the second act of the intellect now: *Judgment.*

Just as a sentence isn't complete unless there is a subject and predicate, something that is talked about, and what is said about it, so too our thoughts are not complete unless there is not just a simple apprehension of something in the world, but a judgment about it. And this is because *thought is judgmental.* Now, by judgmental we do not mean being critical of something in a negative way; we just mean making an affirmation or denial regarding the nature or existence of something. "The cat exists" and "The cat is black" are intellectual affirmations, and thus judgments, and "The cat does not exist" and "The cat is not black" are intellectual denials and are also judgments. These affirmations or denials when expressed in writing or speech are called *propositions* in logic, just as they are called *sentences* in grammar.

The main reason thought is incomplete without judgments is because without judgments, there can be no truth or falsity, and, as we have discussed, logic is primarily about the truth. The simple apprehension of a cat, expressed in our minds as the concept of a cat and in our speech or writing as the word *cat*, is neither true nor false. Only when we affirm or deny something about the concept do we enter into the realm of truth. Aristotle, who, with the help of his teacher Plato and Plato's teacher Socrates, pretty much discovered the science of logic, and he gave us a great definition of truth and falsity, one that helps us see why concepts are not true or false, but only our judgments about them:

Truth and Falsity: To say of what is that it is not, or of what is not that it is, is false, while to say of what is that it is, and of what is not that it is not, is true.

This sounds complex and strange, but it is just Aristotle's way of saying what we all know to be the difference between truth and falsehood. Try to define "false" and "true" in your own words.

Here's a hopefully simpler definition of judgment:

Judgment is the act of affirming or denying one concept of another concept.

The judgments about objects in the world that we make in our minds that are then expressed in propositions and sentences are hopefully accurate descriptions about these objects. When there actually is a cat walking across your path, and you form the correct concepts of "cat," "walking," and "path," and you put these concepts together in the judgment, "The cat is walking across my path," then you have made a true judgment. If, on the other hand, there is no actual cat, but a robot in the form of a cat, then your judgment is false. You could reformulate your judgment to make it more likely to be true by saying, "What appears to be a cat is walking across my path," and this would be a true judgment.

But what if you didn't see the cat because it was two in the morning and pitch black outside, but only heard "meow" coming from somewhere in front of you? Your judgment that there is a cat walking across your path would still be true (if it wasn't a robocat or some other meowing non-cat being) but consider how you came to make that judgment. It would have been split-second thinking, but if you could slow down your mind, it may have gone through these steps. First, "Something in front of me is meowing." Second, "Cats are things that meow." And third, "There is a cat in front of me." In this case, it wasn't just by exercising the first two acts of the intellect that you came to make the judgment, but also the third.

The third act of the intellect is *reasoning*. While it is true that truth and falsity are found in a judgment, the second act of the intellect, and logic is about truth at its core, it is often the case that, as in the example above, an act of reasoning brings our minds to see the truth of things. There are some truths about reality for which reasoning is not needed. For example, there are simple perceptual truths, "That is a cat," that only require experience plus the first and second intellectual acts for us to make a true judgment. There are also truths that are known to us without even needing much experience, but only the meaning of the words, such as, "The whole is greater than the part." These are called "self-evident" truths. There are also truths about morality that are known without the need for argument, such as,

"Murder is wrong" and "Courage is better than cowardice." One could, perhaps, construct arguments that could *prove* some of these propositions to be true, but the truth of these and other fundamental moral propositions are knowable without the need of argument. But aside from perceptual and self-evident truths, all other truths about the world require argumentation to lead the mind to grasp their truth.

The basic structure of reasoning is called a *syllogism*. You will get into the details of the syllogism in the formal logic course, but for now, we can look at it briefly. Let's go back to our favorite cat-walking-across-our-path:

> All meowing things are cats.
>
> Something near me meowed.
>
> Therefore, that thing is a cat.

The first act of the intellect gave you the concepts meowing, near, me, cat. The second act allowed you to put these concepts together into propositions, three of them. But what allowed you to judge that the thing near you is a cat? Yes, you guessed it, the third act! You *reasoned* to it. When you read the first two propositions, you can feel the truth of the third, can't you? That's because the third proposition is true *because* the other two propositions, or premises, are true. In other words, the first two propositions are the *cause* of the truth of the third.

When you push a spoon off a table, you can almost feel the need of the spoon to fall to the ground. That's because you have experienced before the force of gravity as the cause of things falling to the ground when there is nothing below them, and as soon as you pushed the spoon to the edge of the table, gravity did its thing, and you expected it to do so. Similarly, in the syllogism above, the two premises are like gravity — they cause the conclusion to be true, like gravity causes objects to fall.

Now, maybe you are wondering about that syllogism. "It does feel like the conclusion must be true if the first two propositions (called in logic the *premises*) are true, but I'm not sure if the premises are true!" Yes, you are right to wonder. Which of the premises might not be true? Yes, "Only cats meow." What about robocats?! If what appeared to you to be cat was indeed a robocat, then the conclusion, "The thing near me is a cat," would not be true. Good catch! Let's make the syllogism more forceful:

> All things that meow are either cats or things that sound like cats.
>
> The thing near me is a thing that meows.
>
> Therefore, the thing near me is a cat or a thing that sounds like a cat.

Unless there are beings other than cats and robocats that meow, I think we have what's called a *valid* and *sound* syllogism. *Valid* means that the logic is forceful, and *sound* means that the premises are true. Here's a syllogism with invalid logic but true premises. Although the conclusion, in this case, is true, it's not true *because* the premises are true:

> All cats are animals.
>
> Whiskers is an animal.
>
> Whiskers is a cat.

It turns out that your pet cat is named Whiskers, so the conclusion of this syllogism is true. But can you see that what makes it true is *not* the two propositions that precede it? Why not?

Reasoning is the act of the intellect by which the mind is led to a judgment of the truth of a proposition based upon knowing the truth of other propositions.

Reasoning is the act of the intellect by which the mind is led to a judgment of the truth of a proposition based upon the truth of other propositions.

Here's another way of putting all this by the philosopher Peter Kreeft[1]:

These three logical entities answer three different questions, the three most fundamental questions we can ask about anything:

1. **A term answers the question *what* it is.**
2. **A proposition answers the question *whether* it is.**
3. **An argument answers the question *why* it is.**

1. "What are we talking about?" "Man."
2. "What are we saying about it?" "That man *is* mortal."
3. "Why is it mortal?" "Because man is an animal, and all animals are mortal, therefore man is mortal."

Terms, propositions, and arguments reveal three different aspects of reality:

1. **Terms reveal *essences* (*what* a thing is).**
2. **Propositions reveal *existence* (*whether* a thing is).**
3. **Arguments reveal *causes* (*why* it is).**

[1] Kreeft, Peter, *Socratic Logic: First Edition* (South Bend, IN: Saint Augustine's Press, 2004), 30 & 33.

	1st ACT OF MIND	2ND ACT OF MIND	3RD ACT OF MIND
NAME OF ACT	Understanding	Judgment	Reasoning
MENTAL PRODUCT	Term	Proposition	Argument
LINGUISTIC EXPRESSION	Word or Phrase	Declarative Sentence	Paragraph
EXAMPLE OF EACH	"Man," "Mortal"	"Socrates is a man."	All men are mortal. And Socrates is a man. Thus Socrates is mortal.
STRUCTURAL PARTS	None	Subject Term and Predicate Term	Premises and Conclusion
QUESTION ANSWERED	What it is	Whether it is	Why it is
ASPECT OF REALITY	Essence	Existence	Cause
GOOD WHEN	Clear or unambiguous	True	Valid
HOW ACHIEVED	Definition of terms	No one way	Rules of Logic
BAD WHEN	Unclear or ambiguous	False	Invalid
QUESTION TO HABITUALLY ASK	What do you mean? (Define your terms.)	What is your point? (State your conclusion.)	Why? (Prove it.)

Okay, now that you've seen the big picture, it's time to get into the first act of the intellect. Here we go!

Think for yourself...

Answer these:

1) List the three acts of the intellect.
2) What's a concept?
3) What does *simple apprehension* mean?
4) What is judgment?
5) What is reasoning?

Ponder these:

6) When we judge one concept to be related to another, such as, "The cat is black," how do we know if our judgment is true?

7) When we talk to each other, we use words, which, as you learned, are signs of concepts, and concepts are signs of things in the world. But though the world is the same for everyone, our concepts are not in the world but in our own minds. How can we communicate with each other if we're all in our own private conceptual worlds?

LESSON 4: *Understanding Understanding: An Introduction to the Categories*

Now that we have talked about what logic is, why it's important and valuable, and the logical big picture, it's time to delve into material logic proper. Recall that we distinguished material from formal logic in terms of the three acts of the intellect. The second and third acts of the intellect are studied in formal logic and the first act in material logic. This is because formal logic is more concerned with the *structure* of our thinking, while material logic is more concerned with the *foundation* and *content* of our thoughts. Formal logic asks and answers the questions: "What makes an argument valid?" and, "Is that argument valid?" While material logic asks: "What makes a thought accurate to reality?" and, "Is that concept in our minds accurate to reality?"

Material logic is thus more *philosophical* than formal logic. Philosophy is the "love of wisdom" (from the Greek roots *philo,* meaning love, and *sophos,* meaning wisdom). Material logic is less interested in the art and science of making valid arguments than in understanding how it is we can think at all, which requires an inquiry into how we use words to communicate to ourselves and others about reality.

A non-philosophical approach to, say, mathematics would focus on learning formulas and solving equations, and ask questions like, "What is the best way to figure out the answer to this numerical or algebraic problem?" and, "How do we know we have the right answer?" A philosophical approach would focus on the nature of quantity and number, and ask questions like, "What is a number?" "What is a point and a line?", "How can numbers, which don't change, exist in the world of changing things?", and "Does a perfect circle exist only in the mind, while in the material world there are only imperfectly circular things?"

Another way to look at the meaning of philosophy is in terms of the *stages of learning*. You are now in the logic stage of learning, preceded by the grammar stage and to be followed by the rhetoric stage. The grammar stage is all about "what is this?" questions, matters of fact. Your mind is a sponge for knowledge during this time, and you are building a reservoir of good, true, and beautiful images, stories, facts, and ideas. The logic stage is all about asking "why?" in matters of *relationship*. Your mind in this stage immerses itself in the reservoir of knowledge you built in the grammar stage and looks at all the facts, stories, information and truths and tries to see how they are all related to each other. You want to know, most of all, not just *that* something is, but *why* it is, the cause of it being *that*, and not *this*. In the rhetoric stage that beings roughly in high school, you try to put back together what you pulled apart in the logic stage, and you work on seeing and expressing the *whole*, but in a new light, the light of *wisdom* that comes from having looked carefully at the relationships among the parts.

So, let's now return to our first material logic question. What makes a thought accurate to reality? How do I know that, for example, when I think of "cat" in my mind, what's in my mind is at least similar, if not the same, as the actual cat walking down my path? Well, as in philosophy, one question leads to another, and another, and another. And usually the question you're trying to ask can't be answered unless a prior, more fundamental question is asked. So, before we can answer whether my thoughts are accurate to reality, we first have to ask: "What is reality?"

The Categories

Now, this question is perhaps *the* philosophical question underlying all others, aside from "Why is there something other than nothing?" Since this is not an introduction to philosophy course, we're not going to delve that deep! What we need to ask for the purposes of material logic is this: "What is reality insofar as it can be *thought*?" We can't think of all of reality at once, and we can see this in the fact that our thoughts are always of one thing or another, and one thought after another. And we speak and write one sentence at a time, one after another. So, another way we can think about this is: "What are the fundamental *categories* of being?" A category is another word for division, so what we are asking is how is reality or "being" divided up so that we can think about it?

Aristotle, in the fourth century B.C., wrote a book to answer this question called, you guessed it, the *Categories*. Another synonym for category is *predicate*, a word you are familiar with from grammar. A predicate is literally "something said about" (from the Latin *dicere*, to say), and that's why in a sentence we have the predicate, that which is said about something, and the subject, the something which we're talking about. So, a category is what can be said or thought about something, and the categories are the various ways we think and talk about things. Believe it or not, you have already studied the categories, but under another name: the parts of speech.

Remember those? Nouns, adjectives, verbs, and more. Did you ever wonder where these come from? Did someone invent them? Were they discovered? When and where and by whom? Well, the parts of speech have been around as long as grammar has been around, and grammar has been around ever since humans reflected on how their language works; the first written grammar studies can be found as early as the fifth century B.C.

When we look at how we use words, we notice that some words, what we call in English, nouns, give a name to beings in the world, persons, places, things, or ideas, while other words give a name to, not the beings themselves, but what they do, what is done to them, how they do what they do, how they appear and how they differ from one another in appearance. These are verbs, adverbs, and adjectives.

We can think about the parts of speech as the parts of reality. Not that there are nouns and adjectives walking around, but that there are beings and qualities or characteristics of beings to which the parts of speech correspond. Now, in logic we are not so much concerned with words as we are concepts, and just as the kinds of words we use are such because the world is the way it is, the concepts we have in our minds are such because they reflect the way the world is. And just as our words are only as meaningful as they point to what exists in some way (even if, like a unicorn, it exists only in the mind), so, too, our concepts are limited to what has being, either real being or mental being. In short, reality determines and limits what we can think about, and what we can think about determines and limits what we can say or write. So, to figure out what our thinking is all about, we need to inquire what the world is like. What is the world like?

It turns out that the world is like the parts of speech! The reason there is such a thing as a noun, and why it's the first and most fundamental part of speech is because there are things in the world that are, well, "nounlike," and they are the primary example of what we mean when we say that something exists. Aristotle called these beings *substances*, which in Latin means "that which stands under or stands firm."

Look around the room you're in, or outside if you're outside, or out the window, if that applies. What you see are substances: the chair, the rock, the flower, your mother or teacher, the sun, the moon, your pet cat. These beings exist, and what's more, they exist *independently*. That means that they don't exist *in another being*, and they don't depend on another being for their present existence; they exist *in themselves*, and not *in another*.

"Don't all things exist independently and in themselves?" Well, yes, if what you mean by *thing* is a *substance*. But there are other beings than substances. They are less "thing-like" than substances, but they are still real. It's just that they are real only because of something more real or more independently real on which they depend. Go (or remain) outside and look at a flower. The flower is certainly real, but what color is it? If it's a rose, it might be red. What about *red*. Is red real? Well, it's real as a color of the flower. And colors are real. But they exist only *in* things, not as separate things themselves, right?

Have you ever met a "red" in the world? I mean, just a *red*. It sounds silly to say! You have never bumped into a "red," but only a red flower, or red truck, or red ribbon, etc. Yet, everything you meet in the world has color, so, color is, in some sense, real. But it is only real because of the substance it depends on and it exists in. Beings like color, shape, and size differentiate one substance from other substances of the same kind. You have a red rose, and you have white rose. The color, as well as other characteristics like size, shape, where it is located, when it is living or was alive, and the position it is in, is what makes each rose, which is the same *as a rose*, that is, in

An accident, but not an *Aristotelian* accident

its *substance*, different. These features of a substance are called *accidents*.

 A ***substance*** answers to the question, "what is it?", exists independently, not depending on another being, and in itself, not in another being.

 An ***accident*** answers the question, "how is it?", exists only in and because of a substance, and makes a substance different from another substance of the same kind.

"Hey, John! I was in an accident yesterday!"
"No, you weren't"
"But look at my arm, it's in a sling!"
"Even if your whole body were in a cast, I'd never admit that you were *in* an accident.
"Why?"
"Because accidents are *in* other things, never the other way around!"
"You Aristotelians are so annoying."

These *differentiating characteristics* are real, real as the roses and other beings in which they depend on for their existence and that cause them to be different from one another. But they are only real *because* of substances. Aristotle called these beings *accidents*. The literal meaning of *accident* in Latin is "that which falls from," and we can understand them as that whose existence "falls from" or "depends upon" the substances in which they inhere. That which answers the question, "how is it?", exists only *in* and *because of* a substance, and makes a substance different from another substance of the same kind, is an *accident*.

Reality is made up of substances and accidents — and nothing else! There is nothing in the world that is not either a substance or an accident, just as, in light of modern chemistry, we would say that there is nothing material that is neither one of the 118 elements (perhaps there are more yet to be discovered!) on the periodic table, or a compound of these elements. Substance, plus the nine accidents that Aristotle enumerated (I think Aristotle got them all, but you can try to find more!), make up the *categories*, the various ways something can exist. And because thought is nothing but the mind's mirroring of reality, the ten categories are also the various ways being can be thought of.

Introducing . . . The Categories!

Denomination	Question	Example(s)
Substance	What is it?	Man, horse
Quantity	How much? How big is it?	Four feet long
Quality	What are its features?	Red, literate
Relation	In what relation is it to something else?	Double, half, born in, daughter of
Location (place)	Where is it?	Under the table, in the library
Time	When is it?	Yesterday, next week
Posture	What is its orientation?	Lying down, slouching
Having (possession)	What does it have?	Has shoes on, is armed
Doing (action)	What does it do?	Cut, shoot
Experience (passion)	How is it acted upon?	Being cut, being shot

Can you think of any more questions we can ask about something that do not eventually derive from or reduce to these questions above? If you thought of the question "why?" you are right! But it's not a category. We will talk about "why" in a later chapter.

Substance, plus the nine accidents that Aristotle enumerated, make up the **categories**, the various ways something can exist and thus be thought of.

Think for yourself...

Answer these:

1) What does it mean for something to be philosophical? Give an example of a philosophical question. Give an example of a non-philosophical question.
2) Can math be philosophical? Explain.
3) What are the three stages of learning? Why wouldn't the study of philosophy be as appropriate for the grammar stage as the logic stage?
4) What's the difference between formal logic and material logic?
5) List and memorize the 10 categories.

Ponder these:

6) Consider the parts of speech and the categories. Can you see how they are related?
7) Why can't "red" or "six feet tall" be a substance? Why can't "human being" or "plant" be an accident?

LESSON 5: *More about the Categories*

Let's dig into the categories in some more detail. We've talked quite a bit about substance, so we'll focus on the nine accidents for this lesson.

Consider these three statements:

"Socrates is a man."

"Socrates is 6-ft tall."

"Socrates is ugly."

What simple questions does each of these statements answer? Take a minute and think before reading on.

The first statement answers the question, "what?" *WHAT IS SOCRATES?* The second statement answers the question, "how much?" *HOW MUCH IS SOCRATES?* The third statement answers the question, "how?" *HOW IS SOCRATES?* (not how he feels or how he is doing, but more fundamental — in what shape, in what form, in what configuration — does he appear).

You'll notice that the answer to the "what" question, a "man," is a noun (for those grammar nerds, it's a predicate nominative — literally, a "saying" that is a "naming"). The answer to the "how many" and "how" questions are adjectives, predicate adjectives, for they come after the "copula" (that which connects), a word you may recognize as a "linking verb" or a "verb of being." What we have in these sentences are three distinct categories, or, what we can say and think about what *is*.

The fact of the matter is that Socrates *is* (or WAS! — we'll pretend we are alive in the 5th century B.C. for this lesson). But we can't really *think* "is" without some sort of concept or image to accompany it. Try it now! Think of "is"! Chances are you added, without even intending it, some concept or image to define *something* that is. When we predicate what is most essential about what *is*, we predicate the category of *substance*, in this case, a *man*. But as composites of form and matter, substances always exist with particular details, what we have called *accidents*, like 6-ft tall and ugly (or pretty or handsome). These are, respectively, the categories of *quantity* and *quality*.

To see that material substances always include accidents, try to think or imagine "man" or "horse." OK, did the man or the horse have a color, a size, a posture, an action, a place? Even if these accidents were there in your imagination, but just fuzzy and indeterminate, they still determined the man and horse in some way. In other words, you really didn't imagine "man" or "horse" as a pure substance, and that's because you *can't*. Why not? Because whatever you can imagine *always* includes accidents, and *that* is because everything that exists and that can be known through your senses is a combination of substance plus accidents. In other words, "man" and "horse" don't exist!

Now, does this mean that "man" or "horse" isn't at all real, only particular men and particular horses? Yes, in one sense, for only men and horses exist in the world, but "man" and "horse" are, nevertheless, real, in the sense that they are the *essence* of every man and every horse. When we think "man" or "horse" there is certainly something real to which our thoughts are corresponding, right? Essence (or substantial form), like "horse," plus a set of accidents, like brown, large, and in the stable, equals a real, existing, particular being. We will talk more about this fascinating topic of what makes something real, and how we know, in the next chapter on concepts. Are concepts real or only in our minds? What is the relation of real particular existing beings to our concepts about them?

So, we have: "A 6-ft tall, ugly man, a teacher, standing in his toga around the ancient Athenian agora (marketplace), talking with some young Aristocrats about the nature of virtue, and being questioned by them." Guess what — we've got all ten categories in this sentence! Can you find them all? Take a few moments and give it a shot.

We've already talked about Socrates' substance, quantity, and quality (man, 6-ft tall, and ugly). Let's proceed to the others in the order of the words in the sentence.

"A teacher": You might think this description is also of a substance, since teacher is a noun. But is "teacher" the essence of Socrates? It does answer the question, "What is Socrates?", but it does not tell us what he is *essentially*, what his substantial form is. What it does tell us is his *relation* to another. You can think and understand "man" without thinking about any other substance or accident, but you can't understand the meaning of "teacher" without including the meaning of "student," and the same for all other relations, such as father-son, mother-daughter, doctor-patient. Unlike substance, quantity, and quality, all the other accidents are in some way *related* to other beings, other substances or accidents, while substance, quantity, and quality are non-relational. The category *relation* is essentially a relation, while the other relational accidents are essentially some other attribute, and only indirectly a relation. Substance, quantity, quality, and relation are *intrinsic* to the being they describe, while the other accidents are more or less *extrinsic*.

A 6-ft tall, ugly man, a teacher, is standing in his toga around the ancient Athenian agora (marketplace) and talking with some young aristocrats about the nature of virtue, and being questioned by them, at 4pm.

"Talking": This is obviously not a substance, and we can see this grammatically, since it is a verb and not a noun. Talking describes, not what Socrates is, but what he is *doing*. This is the category of *action*.

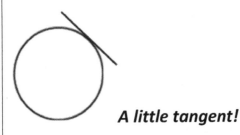

A little tangent!

The fundamental action of all beings is simply to exist. It's a strange example of an action, of course, but to exist is to be *in act*, as opposed to be only in *potency* (we'll be discussing these terms later). Before there is another action by a substance, that substance must first exist. But this "action" is not an accident, like all other accidents. Can you think of why? As we know, accidents can't exist by themselves, but only as parts of a substance, which exists in itself. So, you can say that substances are what make accidents exist, but not vice-versa. But what makes substances exist? Wait for it … the act of existence! The "is-ness" of things is even more fundamental than the "whatness" of things, which is more fundamental than the "muchness" or "howness" or "relatedness" of things. So, existence is so basic that it is *before* substance, and so not even one of the categories. It is like a meta-category.

It is the categories of substance and accident that determine and limit and particularize the act of existence to produce actually existing beings. To see that existence can't "fit" into the categories, try to imagine or think "existence" as a substance. You can't! It's too BIG for substance, let alone an accident! If we can't think it, it's not a category, but this is certainly not to say that existence doesn't exist.

In some religions, the being *who is the very act of existence* is understood to be God.

Okay, back to the category of action. Action is like the category of relation in that an action of a being always relates to the outside world, to other beings, to a lesser or greater extent. There are two types of actions: intransitive and transitive. *Intransitive* actions begin in the actor or agent, and end in him or her or it, that is, the action does not go outside the agent. Consider walking, swimming, or thinking — these actions remain within the person, even though, as all actions, they have some relation to the outside world. *Transitive* activities begin in the agent but end in or affect something other than themselves. "Trans" in Latin means *across*, so these actions go across from the agent to another. Consider "talking to the aristocrats" or "hitting the ball" or "cutting another's hair."

The kinds of actions of which a substance is capable are determined by the nature of the substance. For example, a human being, unlike a fish, is capable of thinking, and that's because a human being is a "rational animal" while a fish is not.

 Intransitive actions begin in the actor or agent and end in him or her or it, that is, the action does not go outside the agent into another object or agent.

 Transitive activities begin in the agent but end in or have an effect on something other than themselves.

"In his toga": This category, *"having"* or *"wearing,"* is perhaps the most *extrinsic* of all the accidents, with quantity being the most *intrinsic*. To see this, try to imagine, say, a horse without any quantity! Now try to imagine it with quantity, but with, say, no color. It's a little easier right? A sort of geometric horse! Quantity is more intrinsic to the substance, and you can see this in your inability to imagine it without it. Now consider "having/wearing"

— you can easily imagine a horse without a bridle, or a man without armor, or a child without shoes on. Why is having/wearing a category then? Well, for Aristotle, our customary appearance, tools, outfits, etc., although not literally a part of our bodies (unless, of course, you're Wolverine!), is still so related to us that he deemed it a basic category of being, one not reducible to any other. should really be considered an accident of all beings, since it is so external or extrinsic, unlike quantity, to the being it describes.

"Around the ancient Athenian agora": This is *where* Socrates is. Every substance is located somewhere or other, and so "where" is one of the "sayables/thinkables" about the "be-ables." This category really brings out the extrinsic nature of several of the accidents, as, obviously, the agora is not *in* Socrates, but the other way around. Yet, where something is is certainly something very connected to its being. Substances are not isolated hermits in their own private worlds but are intrinsically related to other beings (relation), and to a particular location, even though a change of location, "I'm in the house now," does not affect a substance as directly or intrinsically as much as a change in relation, "I'm a father now!", or a change in quantity, "I gained twenty pounds!"

"And being questioned by them": If you've taken some Latin, you may recall the "passive voice" of verbs. This is the grammatical way of denoting an action in which the subject of the sentence *receives* the action, instead of giving or doing it. So, in this sentence, Socrates is receiving the action of being questioned, while the Aristocrats are doing the action of asking him questions. This is the category of *experience,* or *passion* (*passion* is the Latin for suffering, which is another way of saying receiving something).

All beings are always in action in some respect, even if it's just the action of their metabolism digesting food! Similarly, all beings are also always receiving some action, even if it's just the action of gravity on our bodies, being observed by another. Whenever we reflect upon ourselves in our daydreaming, we are both doing the action of reflecting, and receiving the action of being reflected on — a simultaneous action and passion.

"At 4pm": Just as every being is located in a place, so is it situated in a particular time, a *"when."* You might say that the discipline of history is the study of the accidents of action, passion, and time: What did humans do or have done to them in the past? Aristotle defined time as "the measure of change according to the before and after." Sounds weird but think about it a little. Makes sense, huh? Would there be change or motion without time? Would we be able to detect time without something changing or moving, even if it were just the changing thoughts we experience in our minds? If time describes a motion, then you can see why it's usually an adverb, which describes verbs. "I ran at 4pm": "at 4pm" is an adverbial prepositional phrase describing the verb "ran."

Well, that's it for the accidents — for now ...

Think for yourself...

Answer these:

1) Write a sentence and include all the categories in it, like the one I wrote about Socrates.
2) Now take that same sentence and label the parts of speech. Can you see the connection between the parts of speech and the categories?
3) Which of the accidental categories are intrinsic to substance?
4) How is existence an action? Why is it a weird one?

Ponder these:

5) Are the thoughts in your mind substances or accidents? Why?
6) What category are numbers and geometrical shapes in? Are they substances?
7) Do you think "being looked at" is a passion? It doesn't really affect the substance looked at, does it?
8) What would a world that was missing one or more of the nine accidents be like? Choose one or more to remove from the world and imagine it. What would a world without substances be like?

LESSON 6: *Form and Matter*

Substantial Form

It's one thing to be *told* by your teacher that being is made of substances and accidents. It is another thing to *understand why* being is like this. That's what it means to be philosophical. So, let's inquire!

What makes something a substance and not an accident? Why is a cat a substance, but the black of its fur, and even the fur itself, not? According to the classical tradition, what makes something a substance is also what makes it identifiable by the intellect as *this* and not *that*. When we have a concept of "cat" in our minds, it is because there is something knowable about the essence of the cat, distinct but not separate from all the accidents of the cat, like its color and place. What is it that makes this dark being walking across my path a cat? It's not its color, which could be white and it would still be cat; it's not its size, for big or small, it's still a cat; and it's certainly not whether it's doing the action of meowing right now or not.

That which makes the cat a cat is something called in the classical tradition its *substantial form*. When we encounter a cat and think "cat," it's because we have formed a concept that matches the substantial form of the being we have encountered. In fact, it is the substantial form of the cat that is now in our mind — not the cat itself of course! (In the next chapter we will discuss how things in the world "get into our minds"). It's not a copy of the cat, or a picture of it, in our minds, but the cat itself, though without its *matter*. If it weren't somehow the cat itself we were knowing, but only knowing the idea or concept of *cat* in our minds, then we would be stuck knowing our own minds, and not the world outside of them. We'll talk more about this in the next chapter.

So, what is a substantial form? Today, we tend to think of the word *form* in terms of shape or structure, in a geometrical manner: The form of the building is rectangular. But this is not the classical, philosophical understanding of the word. Form, to the ancients, meant the holistic appearance of something, how something shows its whole self to human beings, the essential "whatness" of a thing. These are different ways of saying that form is that which allows us to distinguish and categorize things in various ways. We might think that form is only a pattern of the material parts of something, and so can be seen immediately by the senses, especially by our eyes, but when we think about it, form is more than that.

Even though form is manifested to us in matter, and therefore we discern it initially through our senses, it is more than the present appearance of something, as the following example shows: Consider a living cow, and now consider this same cow that, in the next moment, has just died, such that the dead cow still looks pretty much like it did when alive, as it still has all the cow cells intact. What is the difference between the living cow and the dead cow? We could say that the dead cow is still a cow, but just no longer alive. But is the dead cow still a cow?

If what makes a cow a cow, and what makes anything anything, is that which holds all the cow parts together and enables it to act like a cow, then when the cow died, what happened? We know that as soon as an animal dies, it begins to decompose — de-compose, that is, fall apart, however slowly. When the cow died, it no longer had that which was keeping its parts together, that is, what made it a cow was gone, and it became just, and please excuse the crudity of the expression, a heap of cow cells, no longer united together into a cow. In other words, a dead cow no longer has the substantial form of a cow, and so, is no longer a cow. For the substantial form of a cow is that which makes it a cow, and with its matter, its flesh and bones, disunified, that form is no longer present.

Form and Essence

But we can understand what form and substantial form are from non-living beings as well. Consider water. We know from chemistry that water is a compound, a molecule made from two hydrogen atoms and one oxygen atom. But the "whatness" of water is not reducible to these atoms, for nothing in these atoms is really like water. Water, we might say, is its own thing. It has its own form. So, it would not be correct to identify the substantial form of water as merely H_2O, although this accurately describes water, for this is merely a description of its accidents, its chemical structure, the accident of *quality*, which is not the same as its substantial form. It's like saying that a human being is 75% water and 25% other compounds. Although this is true, is this what a human being really *is*?

So, *form* is that which makes something to be in some way that differentiates it from other somethings. *Substantial* form is that which makes something to be, not just in *some way*, but *essentially*. We can see from this definition that both accidents and substance are forms, with accidents, like the form of blackness of *this* cat, making the cat to be different from some other cats, and the form of "catness," making the animal walking across my path a cat and not a dog.

 Form is that which makes something to be in some way that differentiates it from other somethings.

 Substantial form is that which makes something to be, not just in some way, but *essentially*.

I used the word *essentially* to differentiate substantial from accidental form. I hope you're now wondering what the word *essen-*

tial means! We do use this word quite often, and we think we know pretty much what we mean when we use it. We say, "The essence of the matter is that I lost my keys, so stop talking about the weather!" or "The essence of education is learning how to think, and to pursue the true, the good, and the beautiful, not being told what to think and just preparing for a career" or "The essence of life is to find one's purpose, not merely to live a long time." What we mean by *essence*, then, is the primary meaning, or deepest heart, or what is most central, or the utmost importance, or the definitive core. It is that which remains when we put aside or look through what is merely *accidental*, *accidental* meaning, well, non-essential! So, how do we know what is accidental and what is essential in order to discover the essence of a being?

Form, Matter, and Prime Matter

To answer this question, we need to introduce what is perhaps the most *essential* distinction in all of philosophy, the distinction between form, which we have already discussed, and *matter*, which we have not, though we have used the term. It will surprise you to know that to the classical mind, matter, which we tend to think of as, at the most basic level, the essential stuff of things, and that which is most knowable (think of chemistry and physics), is *not* really anything in itself and is entirely unknowable! Rather, it is *form* which is most essential and knowable.

We could spend an entire year just on the nature of matter and form, and how the natural world can be analyzed and understood in these terms, but for our present purpose, we only need to discuss these as they relate to material logic. In the next chapter, we will see how the process by which concepts are formed in the mind involves *abstracting* the form from matter in the beings we encounter, but for now, we need to get a better handle on what form and matter are.

According to the classical mind, every being that can be sensed with our five senses is a composition of form and matter.

Consider Michelangelo's statue of David. What is it? Well, at the most basic level, it's a piece of marble. Before he chiseled it, it was marble, and after his masterpiece was complete, it was marble. And it still is marble today. But of course, it's different from every other piece of marble. It has been shaped into an image of David. In this example, the matter of the statue is marble, and the form is the image of David. You might say that the form of David was in Michelangelo's mind, and after the statue was completed, that form was imposed upon the marble matter of the statue.

But what about the block of marble, before Michelangelo chiseled it? Is it just matter? You might think so based upon what you just read, but consider it more carefully. Since the marble can be seen and touched, it must be *something*. Since it exists as a *something*, as a being, it must, if the classical view is correct, have a substantial form, and thus be composed of matter and form. What is the matter, then, of the slab of marble?

Well, it is, literally no-thing. Matter, when we get down to it at the most basic level, doesn't exist, for without form, it wouldn't have any characteristics or properties, what we have called *accidents*. It is form that causes something to be a something (substantial form), and to be like *this* and not like *that* in how it exists (accidental forms). It is the matter that makes the substantial and accidental forms visible and tangible and particular.

So, in the case of the marble slab, the form is "marbleness" and the matter is, well, unnameable. It is just that primordial "stuff" that the form of marbleness is imposed upon so that marbleness (the essence of the marble slab) can be an actual, particular, visible and tangible marble slab. This primordial stuff is called *prime matter*.

Consider another example. A brick house. I think you can tell me now what the matter is of this house. Yes, the bricks. Can you see why matter is not enough to account for the being of the house? There must be some other principle or component of the house to explain why the bricks are arranged the way they are. The bricks themselves are just bricks, not a house. That other component (which is not any of the bricks, or even all of them together, so it's weird to call it a component) is the form, in the case "houseness." When we put houseness and bricks together, form and matter, we get a house.

Now consider what happens when the house gets demolished. The matter remains, the bricks, but the form has disappeared. It is no longer a house but now just a pile of bricks. Perhaps now the form is "pileness"! And again, what about just one of the bricks? It's not pure matter, is it? No, it's a combination of matter and form, for it's a something, a brick. The matter is the unnameable stuff upon which "brickness" is imposed.

Let's now go even further into the brick. Each brick is made of clay or something like clay, and clay itself is a composite of minerals, which are reducible to elements, the elements on the periodic table. Each element is just a kind of atom. So, are atoms pure matter? Well, this is a tricky question. We know that atoms are structured a certain way, that is, they each have a form that accounts for its properties. So, every atom is itself made of form and matter. What is the matter of an atom? Each atom is made of parts, like protons and electrons. Are these then "prime matter" with no form? Well, if these parts are a *this,* a *something,* a *being,* then they themselves must have a form, a structure, a set of properties, and this form must itself be imposed on some sort of matter. What, then, is prime matter?

I think you can begin to see that for Aristotle prime matter itself isn't a something, but only a *principle* of something, a certain *potential* for something to be. A something can only be if it is has properties (accidents) and a nature (substantial form) that shapes, determines, or *actualizes* the matter into an existing being. The marble was *potentially* a statue of David, but only was *actually* a statue of David after the form in Mickey's mind was imposed on the matter. But without the matter, the marble in this case, there would also be no statue!

Form alone, such as the idea of David in Mickey's head, doesn't make a something. And matter alone doesn't make anything something either. The properties that constitute an atom of, say, iron, are just abstract properties without any particular reality unless these properties are imposed on some sort of primordial "stuff," stuff that doesn't exist until united with or actualized by these properties.

> **Matter** by itself isn't a something, but only a principle of something, a certain potential for something to be.

What about plants and animals? They too are made of matter and form. Let's take a cat. What is a cat? It's certainly a collection of organic material, of cells. But so are all other animals. So what makes *these* cells a cat, and another collection of cells a dog? Yes, it's the form. "Catness" plus "cells" (and cells plus prime matter!) equals a cat! But here we go again. Are the cells pure matter without form? No! Because each cell has a specific structure and set of properties. We could say that each cell is a combination of organic "protoplasm" (literally, "first stuff") plus a certain arrangement of the protoplasm into, say, a heart cell, or a brain cell. What about the protoplasm? Well, it's made of atoms. Are those pure or prime matter? I'll let you finish the thought!

We ultimately always get down to some unnameable, unsensible "prime matter" that doesn't exist actually, but only potentially, gaining existence only when "actualized" by a certain form. And remember that this form doesn't exist by itself, but only in conjunction with some matter upon which it can be imposed.

So, I think we can more easily see now why every being that is a substance (existing independently and not in or because of another being) is a combination of, not just form and matter, but *substantial* form and *prime* matter. A human being is a substance, and so is composed of the substantial form "human" plus matter, in this case, that "stuff" that can be made into a human, namely, cells. But these cells are also composed of form and matter. A tree is a substance and so is composed of the substantial form "tree" plus the matter, tree cells, which are also composed of form and matter. Marble is a substance and so is made of the form "marble" plus, ultimately, that nameless pure potency that Aristotle called "prime matter."

Back to the *categories* to finish the lesson. A baby human has the same substantial form as an adult human, namely, "humanity", and the same kind of matter as an adult human, human cells. So, what is the difference between a baby and an adult human? Can you look back at the categories and figure out the answer? If the baby has the same substantial form as her mother, then she must differ only in *accidental forms*, namely, size (she's smaller), quality (her shape is a bit different), and action (she doesn't yet have the ability to, say, read).

Another way to understand the difference between an adult human and a baby human is in terms of matter and form. A six-month-old baby has the same *form* as a thirty-year-old woman, the form of humanness, but the matter is quite different. The baby is *actually* a human because she shares the same form, but only *potentially* an *adult* human, for her matter has not yet "caught up" to the fullness of her human form. This catching up is what we call growth. It is the same with an acorn. What is the substantial form of an acorn? (hint, it's not an acorn).

In sum, prime matter is — not atoms! — but literally "no-thing," for being the underlying "stuff" of all things, it has the potential to become anything. Prime matter has no physical appearance, quality or quantity. Prime matter cannot even be thought of as separate from form. Form is what allows prime matter to become a substance and vice versa. For instance, all of the elements on the Periodic Table (such as iron, gold, silver, mercury, etc.) can be thought of as comprised of form plus prime matter. The thing that differentiates the elements from each other is their form. Silver and gold are composed of the same prime matter, as are all things, but have different substantial forms. Form and prime matter constitute the substance of any and every object, and the substantial form plus the accidents (the nine categories other than substance) give the substance a physical reality that is knowable, that is, we can form a concept in the mind about it.

And it is to the concept that we now turn.

Think for yourself...

If a chair or a house were a substance, it would have a substantial form. Does it? Consider the categories. What makes a chair different from a piece of wood? Is a chair substantially different from a piece of wood?

Answer these:

1) What is substantial form?
2) What is form?
3) What is matter?
4) What is prime matter?
5) What is an essence?

Ponder this:

6) The substantial form of something isn't one of the parts of that something, and it's not just another word for all the parts. If the substantial form is neither one nor all of the parts, what is it and how do we know it exists? How can it exist if it is not a material thing that we can sense?

LESSON 7: *The Concept*

We've talked *a little* about the concept of *concept* — so to speak. Let's review:

- A **concept** is just a subject or a predicate, but considered, not as a word or phrase written or spoken out loud, but as something in the mind.
- The formation of a concept, or the *simple appre-hension* of what something is, is **the first act of the intellect**.

We've talked *quite a bit* about what concepts are *about*, what they depend on, and what they make present to our minds, namely, reality. It's important to see why we discussed what reality is before our present discussion about what concepts are and how they come into existence. The reason is that reality causes the concepts in our minds, and so to know better the effect, the concept, we must first understand the cause, reality.

It is a basic principle of philosophy that every effect has a cause, and the cause must be equal to or greater than the effect. For example, the cause of the air being hot (the effect) in the summer is, first and foremost, the sun (the cause). The air itself is also a cause, in the sense that it has the *potential* to be hot — if it didn't, no matter how hot and close the sun was to it, the air wouldn't get hot! But the *active* cause of the heat in the air is the sun.

It would be much harder to understand the nature and cause of the heat in the air if one did not already understand something about the nature and cause of the sun, the heat's cause. Similarly, since concepts are caused by reality, as well as our minds, it was helpful for us to examine the categories of reality before delving deeply into concepts.

Now, concepts are also caused by the human mind, so what we need to do in this lesson is to examine the relationship of the human mind to reality, and how out of this "causal relationship" the concept is 'effected" (a cool word that just means, "made into an effect.") Before we get into some detail about how concepts are formed in our minds, let's talk a little more about what they are. When we want to know about something in detail, we use our senses, especially our eyes, and examine it closely. Science takes this empirical ("sensory") examination even further by enhancing the detail and accuracy of our sensory knowledge with instruments, such as microscopes, telescopes, and meters (thermometers, barometers, etc.). But can everything we want to know about be investigated in this way?

Can you think of something in your experience that your senses or even scientific instruments can't observe?

Consider numbers. Arithmetic is the science of numbers, and you learned arithmetic in your early years of schooling. How do we first know about numbers? We look at objects around us and count them, and from this counting we learn about numbers. But do we *see* the numbers with our eyes? Look at your hands and count your fingers. You don't actually see the numbers 1, 2, 3, 4, and 5 on your hand, do you?

What you are considering in your mind when you see and count your fingers is the intellectual *category* of quantity, expressed in this case in the quantity of fingers you have on your hand. What you *see* are the fingers. What you are *considering in your mind* is the accident of quantity. And when you consider, or think, of the quantity of your fingers, ignoring for the moment their shape, color, and the fact they are part of your hand (which is part of your body, which is, together with all that you are, a substance, a human being), you are not actually "seeing" the number 5, but *thinking* of it.

The number 5 doesn't exist as a particular being (*Hi, I'm the number 5! —* nope!), certainly not as a real, existing substance, like a cat or a piece of cheese. It is also not really an accident, like the red in the red dress. Your hands do exist, and they exist as "five-fingered," which is an accident (quantity) of your hand, but the number 5 itself doesn't exist as either a substance or an accident of a material being, but only in your mind as a *concept*. So, the most accurate way to describe a concept is to call it an *accident of the human mind* (which has a material component, the brain, but is not, for the classical philosopher, only the material brain).

Yet, things like your hand have quantity, as we learned when we discussed the Categories, which can be counted and measured; so, numbers, although they don't technically exist as particular material beings or accidents of material beings, are not just unreal fantasies of the human mind with no connection to the real world. We can't come up with new or different numbers, and we can't change them — they are what they are! This suggests that numbers are in some way independent of human thoughts and desires, and objective in some mysterious way, doesn't it? We do have a science of numbers — arithmetic — so numbers must be knowable and discoverable. In short, there are objects of human experience that are not material or sensible, but exist in some way in the real world, and are knowable. Mathematical objects, including numbers, are just such objects. Precisely how they exist and "where" is a question for philosophy, not logic, so we'll move on.

Are there other non-material existing realities besides numbers? What about truth, goodness, and beauty? Do these exist? Can they be known? Well, this is a deep philosophical question! We do experience goodness in an act of, say, kindness; beauty in the beholding of a sunset, and truth in the conviction we feel when we see the necessity of something — 2+2=4, yes, that must be! We can say, logically speaking, that since they are words that have meaning for us, they are concepts, and thus they certainly exist, for concepts exist. The question that logic can't answer is whether there is anything real in the world to which our concepts of truth, goodness, and beauty correspond.

Well, if numbers exist to the extent that they can be discovered by us, are independent of our desires or thoughts, and can't be changed, then perhaps goodness, beauty, and truth also exist! We do have sciences of these, after all. The science of goodness is called ethics; the science of beauty is called aesthetics; the science of truth is called epistemology. What are these sciences studying exactly? Study philosophy and find out!

There are many other examples of seemingly non-sensible and immaterial yet existing and knowable realities — think of virtues (justice, courage), feelings (pain, joy) and deep principles (love, honor). How about your own consciousness, your own sense of self, along with its thoughts and, yes, concepts? Is your consciousness something you can see with your eyes or measure with instruments? But doesn't it exist?

I think we have a justification for accepting at least the possibility of the existence and knowability of things in the world that are not able to be sensed. Perhaps you have figured out that these objects, whatever they are, could not be material substances composed of matter and form. And perhaps you are wondering if they are something like forms alone, without matter. Well, if so, I think you're on to something! Concepts, which are the primary objects studied by logic, as you may also have guessed, are not material substances, and are indeed something like forms without matter! Can form exist without matter? How?

What really *are* concepts? Let's try to answer this by saying what concepts are *not*. Let's use for our example the concept *horse*.

Concepts are not material

A horse is a horse, of course, and is made of matter, flesh and blood, and so is a material being. But a horse, like every other material being, is not just matter, as we have discussed. Instead, according to the classical mind out of which material logic was developed, it is a synthesis of matter and form, or, more pre-cisely, *prime* matter and substantial *form.*

What makes a horse *this* horse on which I ride, and not just an abstract horse in my mind, is its matter. What makes this horse in front of me a *horse* (and not a cat) is its substantial form.

Now, the horse itself, as a synthesis of these two principles of being, is material, but the two principles or components that make up the horse are not in themselves material. What? Matter isn't material? Yes, prime matter isn't made of matter! Remember that prime matter is only *potentially* something real, becoming something actual and material only when it is "actualized" or united with form — prime matter is nothing actual in itself. And substantial form — by itself — is not material either, because it only exists as a particular knowable being when united to matter; in other words, form needs matter, just as matter needs form, to exist in the real world. Form is that which unites to prime matter to become a material being. The substantial form "horse" is not the material being itself, but only what makes the actual running horse on which I am riding a horse and not a cat.

So, what about the *concept* of horse? Well, I think you can see that if "horse" (the form of *this or that* horse) is not material, but only *this or that* horse is material, then the concept of horse certainly can't be material either. Let's try to experience the immateriality of "horse." Think of "horse." Ok, what color is it? How large? What kind of horse? If you could answer any of these questions, then you did not *think* of *horse*, but instead *imagined* a horse. Try again. Don't think of *a horse*, but just horse. Think horse. Horse, not *a* horse. OK. What are you thinking of?

Well, it's hard to say isn't it! You want to say that the horse is brown or black, a certain size, a certain breed, a certain age, etc. Or perhaps you just pictured in your head some sort of generic fuzzy horse-like being with no clear color or determinate size. But if it's really the concept "horse" in your mind, it would have to include and represent *all* horses, not just brown or black ones, not just Mustangs, and certainly not generic fuzzy horses, which don't exist!

As we will discuss in more detail later, the concept in your mind of "horse" is really nothing other than the substantial form of the horse on which you are riding, except "taken out" of the horse and put into your mind! (well, even though it's in your mind, it's still in the horse!) And just as the substantial form, *horse*, is not material, neither is the concept *horse*.

Concepts are not particular

Something that is not particular is universal, and so not limited to or restricted by a particular place or being — like the universe! For instance, laughter is a *universal* sign of something being funny, but saying the words "that's funny" is *particular* to English speakers. Concepts are universal in a slightly different way.

The reason you could imagine *a* horse, but could not imagine *horse*, is because "horse," either the substantial form of horse in every horse, or the concept horse in the mind of anyone who has ever seen a horse, is a *universal*. Opposed to universal is *particular*. These are fancy words for a distinction you already know. It's the good-old grammatical distinction between common nouns and proper nouns. Why do you capitalize proper nouns? Because, like Tigger, there's only one of them, right? They're "special." So, why do you use lowercase for common nouns? Well, they are just ordinary and run-of-the-mill. There's a lot of cats, but only one Tigger. In short, common nouns are universal, and proper nouns are particular.

It's obvious what a proper noun represents and points to — some particular cat or horse or person or city. But what does a common noun represent and point to? That's harder to see. In fact, it's literally impossible to "see" because what it is pointing to and representing is not visible! Can you see why? As we discussed in earlier lessons, only particular beings *exist* in the material world, either as substances, like horses, or accidents, like the brown of the skin of the horse. So, universal beings, like *horse* or *brown*, do not exist in the material world — yet they still exist in the *real* world, which is not necessarily the same as the *material* world. But they don't exist as material substances or material accidents; instead, they exist as the *universal essences* of material substances and material accidents.

How do we know that universals exist? For purposes of logic, we need only posit their existence and nature, for this is all we need in order to study concepts, which are universal. Extensive philosophical argumentation would be needed to treat this question adequately, but we can say a little. Consider the concept *beauty*. We see with our eyes and hear with our ears beautiful paintings and songs. What is it that all the beautiful things we experience have in common? They all to some extent *are* beautiful, that is, they possess the feature or accident of beauty, along with other more substantial features, such as being a sunset or a song.

But none of the beautiful things we encounter *are* beauty itself, for if they were — if, say, horses *are* "beauty," nothing else but horses could be beautiful. So, we could say that things share or *participate* in beauty. Universals are that which particulars have in common so that we can use common nouns, such as horse, or describe them in the same way, as beautiful. If universals weren't real to some extent, more than just mental categories, we wouldn't be talking about the real world when we said that Mozart's music is beautiful, or that this animal is a horse. Does that seem right to you? Is there really no such thing as a horse, as beauty, as goodness, truth, and love? These are all universals, and so if universals don't exist, neither do they.

If there were no universals, there would also be no common nouns. Can you imagine trying to communicate without common nouns? Let's say that you wanted to describe the field of grass over yonder, but you couldn't use the word *grass*. Instead, you would need to describe every blade of grass in all their innumerable differences and minute details, and then give a *name* to each of them, for each blade of grass must be named by a proper noun! I think one of the most compelling arguments for the existence of universals is the mere fact of the existence of common nouns in all the languages of the world since the beginning of human language.

Concepts are not changeable

Our minds constantly change as we think about different things. The mind seems to be the most changing thing there is! So, how can concepts be unchangeable if our concept-full mind is always changing?

Yes, our thoughts come and go, seemingly without rest, and so it is right to say that *our* minds change from one concept to another. But this does not mean that our concepts themselves change. It just means that our minds attend to one concept after another. The concept "red" can never become "not-red," but a lump of red-hot coal can become grey after cooling down. "4" doesn't change, though four living birds can become three living birds if one is shot by a hunter.

 Can you think of anything else besides concepts that are unchangeable?

Material beings change, yes, but not everything about them changes. Remember *the nine categories of accidents*. Consider a horse again. A horse changes its accidents of place and action every time it walks. But the horse remains a horse throughout these changes. Similarly, the concept of horse remains the same in my mind, your mind, and all the minds of all humans throughout time, even though the images in our memory and the memory of others of particular horses may be varied and changing.

Relations between concepts cannot be otherwise (they are necessary).

It is not necessary that you are reading this logic book at some point in the future. Why? Because you very well might not be reading it! If something can be otherwise, it is not necessary. But if you *are* reading the book (and doing it successfully), then it is necessary that you know how to read. And this is because there is a necessary relation between the concept *reading* and the concept *knowing how to read*, such that, the former depends on the latter. If you are reading, then it *must* be the case that you know how to read. And this necessity stems from a prior, more fundamental necessity, namely, that if one is doing some activity more or less successfully, one knows, more or less, how to do that activity.

Mathematics is the study of the conceptual relations of those concepts that have to do with quantity. It doesn't study the "real world" of substances in motion, but only the conceptual world of quantity abstracted or taken out of the real world, just as grammar studies the verbal world. And this is why mathematics and logic are so exact and demonstrable, for all the relations they study are necessary. Grammar is less exact and demonstrable, especially when it gets down to the usage of words, because words are not as unchangeable, universal, and spiritual as concepts, though words are intimately related to concepts.

 Concepts are immaterial, universal, unchanging, and related to each other necessarily.

It is amazing to think how certain and unchanging mathematics is. Consider a triangle. In a triangle, the sum of the interior angles equals 180 degrees. In a circle, every point on the circumference is equidistant from the center. These relations are necessary — they have no choice in the matter — and cannot change. It will never be true no matter how hard I wish it were that 2+2=5.

Think for yourself...

Answer these in your own words:

1) What is a concept?
2) Describe the difference between a word, a concept, and reality.
3) Explain how concepts are: immaterial, unchangeable, and universal.
4) Can you think of any relations in the outside world (neither concepts nor mathematics) that appear necessary? Explain why.

Ponder this:

5) Words and other material things exist "on the outside," in the real world, and so we can see and hear them. Concepts, however, exist "on the inside," in our minds. No one has ever seen a thought — the most we can see are the electrical-chemical impulses in the brain that occur when we think. Yet, we are certainly aware of thoughts! They are real, they exist, and they are not material. Just ponder the way your consciousness of the world is not itself part of the world, yet it is real, even seemingly more real, than the world of matter. After you ponder, write a few sentences about your ponderings.

Lesson 8: *Simple Apprehension, Comprehension, and Extension*

Recall our discussion of simple apprehension a while back. Do you remember what it is? Yes, it's another name for the first act of the intellect, the exercise of which results in a concept in our minds. Remember that judgment, the second act, results in a proposition, and argument, the third, results in a syllogism or some chain of reasoning involving an inference. It's a good time now to go into more depth regarding simple apprehension, and we shall continue along these lines for the rest of the book. In this lesson, we shall first examine how the mind generates a concept, then analyze the parts of a concept (Comprehension), and finally how these parts relate to the outside world (Extension).

Simple Apprehension

Let's return to our friend, the horse. Betty is several feet away from you, yet you are aware of her existence — and she is aware of yours. Somehow, the horse and you are present to each other, though separated by space. How did the horse "get into" your mind, and you into the horse's mind? We use the word *perception* to describe the act of being aware of something. You *perceived* the horse, and the horse perceived you. Perception is an act that only beings with some sort of mind can do, for only minds can take in the outside world and register it, so to speak, on the inside. In short, only animals can become aware of things and thus perform the act of perception.

I know what you are thinking — "How do you know trees and rocks aren't aware of things?" Well, as far as we can tell, one needs sense organs and some sort of nervous system to perceive things. Recall your lessons in biology that explain why this is the case. Now, neither rocks nor plants have sense organs or nervous systems (though the Venus Fly Trap comes close!). Thus, although they can *react* to the outside world — a rock reacts to gravity by falling, a plant reacts to sunlight by heliotropic motion (look it up!) — they cannot *perceive* the outside world. Only animals can do this. Even a sponge "sees" the world, not through the sense of sight, of course, but through some sort of very primitive "touch" sense, by which certain specialized cells register the need to "vomit up" indigestible food in the water.

Well, back to Betty. When you look at the horse, you perceive the horse. When you look away from the horse, you no longer perceive the horse, but something else that your eyes are now focused on. But something remains in your memory of the horse you were looking at, for even when you are no longer looking at the horse, you can picture Betty in your imagination at will and sometimes against your will (Don't think of a horse — you just did!) It's like your eyes took a picture and stored it on the film of your brain.

Let's say you look at other horses of different sizes, shapes, colors, breeds, and temperaments. You now have several images of various horses in your memory. There is something common to and in these images of horses in your mind. The *concept* of *horse*, as distinct from the *image* of *a* horse, is produced in your mind by what is common *to* and *in* these images. Perhaps you can figure out what this common something is, based upon what we learned in previous chapters. Got it yet? … I'll give you a hint — it has to do with matter and form. Yes, the common "something," in both the horse images and all the horses themselves, is the *substantial form* of the horse.

Recall that the substantial form of any substance is that which "actualizes" the matter, and so is, together with the matter, what makes the horse actually exist in the real world, and not just as a concept or a word. The substantial form is also what makes the horse a *horse* and not some other kind of being.

The <u>concept</u> of horse, as distinct from the <u>image</u> of a horse, is produced in your mind by what is common to and in these images.

So, the concept of horse that is produced in your mind is identical to the substantial form of the horse. For, what is common to all particular horses is the substantial form "horse," and what is common to all particular images of horses in your mind is also the substantial form "horse." Now, you might be wondering, how can the form of the horse "get into" your mind? You may also be wondering how something particular, like a horse, can have a form that is universal, and how something universal, like a concept, can even *be in* a particular human mind, let alone how it could enable us to know a particular horse.

Aristotle's book *De Anima* (on the soul) explains in great detail the process by which concepts are formed in the mind from beings in the world. For purposes of logic, we are more interested in the nature of the concept, and less in how the brain and mind (two different but intimately interrelated things according to the classical view) work. But I will give a brief description of Aristotle's account, if only because it's so interesting. We have advanced a lot in our knowledge of the brain since Aristotle's time, and Aristotle got some of his scientific facts and concepts wrong, it seems, but many think Aristotle's understanding of the genesis of concepts is essentially accurate.

We know from modern science that light reflects off objects and enters our eyes through the pupil, then travels through the cornea and lens, finally to "rest" on the retina, where the rod and cone cells translate the refracted light into an electrochemical signal that the optic nerve sends to the brain. Finally, the brain translates this signal into an image, of which the human being becomes aware as an object in his or her environment: "I perceive a cat!"

Notice that in the act of sense-perception, we do not perceive an image as if it were in our brain, but we perceive that to which the image corresponds in our outside-the-brain environment. In other words, we don't say, "I perceive an image of a cat in my brain or mind," but, "I perceive a cat on the grass in front of me." That's because the image mysteriously puts you in contact with that of which it is an image. It's as if you and the cat have become one through the image, such that the cat itself is in your mind, not physically, of course, but imaginatively.

Now, we have an image of the cat in our minds. But, as you know, this is not yet the concept of "cat," because concepts are universal, and the image of "this cat" is quite particular — it's the image of a black kitten, and so couldn't possibly represent or correspond to ALL cats. How could we get the universal concept, cat, from the particular cat and the particular image of the cat?

Well, here's Aristotle's explanation. The substantial form, cat, is mixed with the matter of the cat, and the product of the mixing of the two "ingredients" is what we call a cat. The form, though universal in itself, becomes particularized through being mixed with cat matter (not cat litter!). But the human mind is able to "de-mix" the form from the matter, and this is what produces the concept. The human intellect has the power to "abstract" the universal form from the sensible particulars in which it is hidden.

Mysteriously, the light that reflects off the cat and eventually is transformed by our eyes and imaginations into an image of the cat is also transformed into a concept of the cat. The intellect (not the imagination, Aristotle says) "looks" at the image of this cat in front of me right now, or the various images of cats stored in the memory, and "sees" (by an intellectual "sense") in the image a universal form, one not visible to the eye or audible to the ear. In short, in the image of a cat, it sees *cat*. The intellect turns its gaze away from the accidents (the nine categories) of the cat, it's color and shape and size, and sees what is common to all cats, namely, catness. And now, with our concept of cat produced in our minds, as we are looking at the particular cat in front of us, or afterwards when we recall the cat, we can think, "this is a cat", "that was a cat."

Here's a diagram that might be helpful:

Notice in the above diagram that in the imagination, the image of the horse looks like a horse, but in the intellect, there is no image. This is because the concept of the horse is universal, not particular. It is also because the intellect knows the *meaning* of things in the world, not how they look, or sound, or smell. The meaning of a being is universal and unchangeable and immaterial, so not something the senses or the imagination can know. The meaning of a horse is whatever the essence of a horse is — how would you define the essence of a horse? — and this essence is common to all horses, and so is not any particular kind of horse. Neither is it some fuzzy vague horse shape that can include all horses — for such a shape wouldn't include *any* horses.

The **meaning of a being**, or its **essence**, is universal and unchangeable and immaterial, so not something the senses or the imagination can know, only the intellect, by way of the senses and the imagination.

One additional consideration might be helpful here. It might be thought that the image and concept are just copies of the object, like photographs. This isn't quite right. According to the classical tradition, knowledge entails a *union* of knower and known, whereby the person knowing becomes, in his imagination and mind, the object that he knows. The image in the imagination *just is* the sensible form of the object. The concept in the mind *just is* the substantial form of the object. But there is a difference. The image of the cat is the sensible form of the cat, yes, but *without the matter* of the cat. Otherwise, you'd have an actual cat in your head! Similarly, the concept of the cat is the substantial form of the cat, but universalized. In the cat, "catness" is so mixed with particularity (which is to say, matter) that it can't be seen as a universal by the eyes. But it can be seen to be universal *by the mind*, for the mind is able to *abstract* out the particularity to uncover the universality and meaning within.

An analogy might help. When you read a good book, there are words, sentences, and paragraphs that you can *see*. The meaning of all these words, however, is something we get *through* the words. The words themselves are not their meaning. The words themselves are the sensible signs, and the meaning of each word is something signified by the word, so not the written word itself. One is led to *think* of the meaning by *seeing* the word. Now, when one considers the meaning of the whole book, with all the thousands of words, it is obvious that the meaning is not there in any of the words themselves, or even in all of them together. The meaning is discovered by the *intellect* when it reflects on the meaning of each episode and chapter, each character and action, and then the plot as a whole.

Similarly, neither the horse itself, nor the image of the horse in your mind, is the *whatness* or *essence* of the horse, for the horse and the image of the horse embody and particularize the universal essence, but they do not *fully* express and embody it. You only discover the whatness of a horse in knowing the horse, which is to say, in producing a concept of "horse" that is one with and the same as the substantial form, horse. The concept comes into your mind through experiencing many different horses, but it is not identical to any of the horses, nor to all of them together.

> **Knowledge** entails a *union* of knower and known, whereby the person knowing becomes, through his senses, imagination, and intellect, the object that he knows.

Comprehension

Although concepts are invisible and immaterial, they have "parts." I put *parts* in scare quotes because they are quite unlike the parts of material objects with which you are familiar. They are, rather, *conceptual parts*, parts of the *meaning* of some universal essence. An example or two will help.

What are the parts of the concept "human being"? To discover the answer, one could ask, "What is a human being?" Consider that there is more than one correct answer. I could say, "an animal," and I'd be correct. I could say, "a plant," and I'd be incorrect. But I could also say, "an organism," and I'd also be correct. You can see here that the concept *human being* contains at least two parts, *animal* and *organism*.

Can you see the relation of the two concepts *animal* and *organism*? Which one is "bigger"? Yes, organism is bigger because there are a lot more organisms than there are animals. All animals are organisms, but not all organisms are animals. The group of organisms contains not just animals, but also plants and bacteria (which are, as you may know, considered neither plants nor animals).

So, if we analyze the concept "human being," we find other concepts nested within it, such as organism and animal. The conceptual parts that together make up a larger concept are called "notes." And the collection of notes is what we call the *comprehension* of a concept. Let's try to name all the conceptual parts that make up "human being" and thus discover its comprehension.

We've got the concepts *animal* and *organism*. What's an organism? It's a *living* being, for sure. But what kind of being is a living being? Well, obviously, it's a *material* being. In other words, a being that has a *body*. Are there living beings that are immaterial? Well,

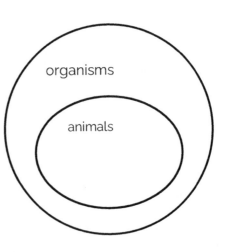

that depends upon one's approach to the world, but if we say there are, like angels or souls, then we would have living beings without bodies, or, spirits. But whether bodily or non-bodily, they are *substances.*

So, we've got some more notes. In addition to *animal* and *organism,* we now have *body* and *substance.* A human being is a substance, a body, an organism, and an animal. If we change these nouns to adjectives, we could say that a human being is a substantial, material, living, and sentient (sentient means "having senses," and that's how we differentiate animals from plants) being. But aren't we missing something? Do you know what else is substantial, material, living, and sentient? A horse. So, what makes a human being different from other animals? According to the classical tradition, a human being is a *rational* animal, meaning, having the capacity for abstract thought and thus free choice.

OK, we've got our notes! When we break up the concept *human being* into its conceptual parts, we get, adjectively speaking, substantial, material, living, sentient, and rational; and in terms of nouns: substance, body, organism, and animal. The noun form of notes are called *genera,* with the singular called a *genus.* You may be familiar with the word *genus* from biology. We will talk about genus in the next chapter when we look at the *predicables,*

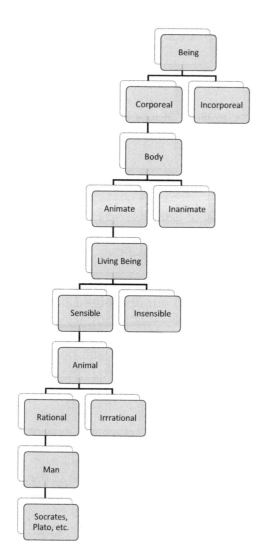

which denote the various relations concepts can have with one another. Here's a helpful diagram to illustrate notes (on the next page). It is called the "Porphyrian Tree," which is named after the ancient Greek philosopher Porphyry.

Notice that at the top of the tree lies the most general concept, "being" or "substance," and as you go down, you narrow the concept down little by little, until you get to "man," below which there are no other concepts or notes. At this point there are just particular men. *Man* is the substantial form of every human being, which, as we have seen, includes other concepts implicitly, such as, animal, living being, body, and substance. There is no smaller category that we can place between man and particular men that is part of man's essence. We could put "male" or "female" or "tall" or "short" or "Chinese" or "Polish" at the bottom of the tree, but these notes, although not insignificant in themselves, are not part of the definition of a human being. What is accidental to a concept does not belong to the comprehension of the concept, only what is essential.

 The **comprehension** of a concept is the description of all the conceptual parts, or notes, of the concept.

But you might be asking, "Male or female and tall or short, and the like, are how human beings actually *exist*, so why are they not part of how we *think* of human beings? Doesn't simple apprehension, the first act of the intellect, take into consideration actual human beings?" Well, to answer your first question, "They are!", and to your second, "Yes!" Simple apprehension includes not only the comprehension of a concept, "What is a human being?", but also to what this concept refers in the real world. The set of actually existing beings in the world, past, present, and future, to which our concepts refer now, in the past, and in the future, is called the *extension* of the concept.

Extension

Do you notice something about the number of notes in each concept as you go up the tree? Compare the concepts *man* and *animal*, for example. Which has more notes? Man does, for it includes animal as well as all the other notes, while animal contains the other notes, but not man. So, as you go up the tree, the comprehension decreases. What about the extension? Let's look at men and animals. Which concept refers to more beings in the world: *man* or *animal*? Right! *Animal* includes all the people in the world, but *people* does not include all the animals. All humans are animals, but not all animals are human. So, as you move up the tree, the extension increases. One can conclude that there is an *inverse relationship* between comprehension and extension.

The more abstract a concept is, the less comprehension there is, but greater is the extension. *Substance* is a very abstract concept — you can see this by the absence of any particular image in your mind when you say the word. There are really no parts making up this concept — no notes. The only "note" above substance would be *being*, but being is so abstract and small in comprehension that it's not even on the Porphyrian tree! Instead, the tree top is substance (or accident, if you were trying to find the comprehension of, say, "red"). But how many substances are there!? WAY more than the amount of human beings. Every atom, every grain of sand, every molecule of water is included in the extension of water, as well as every human being. So, extension is the sum total of all beings in the world to which a concept refers.

Extension is the sum total of all beings in the world to which a concept refers.

Okay, so we perceive beings, become aware of them, and then through the images and concepts that are produced by our imaginations and intellects, we come to understand them, to grasp their meaning. But how do we really know what the meaning of a being is? How can we *define* a being? Yes! These are the logical next questions you should be asking. And so to definition and "the predicables" we now turn.

Think for yourself...

Answer these in your own words:

1) What is perception? What kinds of beings are able to perceive?
2) Describe how an image is formed of some being in the world.

3) Describe how a concept is formed of some being in the world.
4) What is the difference between an image and a concept?
5) What is the relationship between a concept and the substantial form of a being?
6) What is comprehension? What are notes?
7) Give the comprehension of: a) a horse b) a rock c) a plant d) a chair e) the color red.
8) What is extension?
9) How are comprehension and extension related?.

Ponder these:

10) How is it that through an image and concept we can know the being itself, not just a copy of the being? How could we really know that we weren't just knowing a copy of the horse, say, when we think of horse? How could we know that we really contact the real world with and in our minds? What if we do not and cannot contact the real world, but only copies of it in our minds?
11) Are there concepts that have comprehension but no extension? Examples?

LESSON 9: *Reality in Relation*

The Predicables

Simple apprehension produces a concept by which we know the essence of a being. The expression in words of the essence of a being, which is to say, its comprehension, is called a *definition*. To define is to "de-limit" or put a limit on something. The limit we put on a being when we define it is twofold: we separate it from all other essences to express its uniqueness, and we indicate that it is a definite and bounded, not vague and unlimited, reality. According to the medieval theologians, the essence of everything created can be defined, because it's being is limited and finite. But God's essence cannot be defined by humans because his being is unlimited and infinite.

Definition is the completion of the first act of the intellect, for once we have defined a being, we can then make accurate judgments about it (second act), and infer other judgments about it (third act). In order to define something, we need to know its comprehension, but we also need to know the relation of the notes to each other, and this we do by means of the *predicables*. We will take on definition in the next chapter, for we need to understand the predicables before we can understand definition.

Recall our discussion of the categories, which are the various ways we can think and speak about beings. Thinking and speaking about something is to *predicate*, and that's why every sentence we speak or write has a subject, the "about which" we say something, and the "predicate," the "that which" we say about the something. So, the categories could also be called the predicates, that is, what we can say about beings based upon the various modes in which beings can exist. We can talk about their substantial form — cat, horse, or human — or we can talk about their accidents — black, running, or in-the-room. So, if the categories are also the predicates, what are the predic-*ables*?

The predicables are the five possible relationships a predicate can have to its subject. Predicables, like predicates, are always universal, meaning that we can describe many different beings all at once with them. For example, "John is an animal." Animal is the predicate, and it describes John, but because it is a universal, think of all the other beings it also can be predicated of. Billions!

 The **predicables** are the five possible relationships a predicate can have to its subject.

To help us understand the predicables, let's look at grammar again, like we did before to help us understand the categories. The categories, as you may remember, correspond to the parts of speech. Substance = noun, accidents = adjectives, verbs, adverbs, prepositional phrases, etc. (depending on which accident it is; for example, the accident of *action* corresponds to *verbs*, while the accident of *quantity* corresponds to *adjectives*).

Now, there is another way to analyze sentences grammatically, and that is to look at the *syntax* of the sentence, which is a word that means the relationship that the words have to each other, including their function in the sentence. "Syntactical terms," then, are different than the parts of speech, and you may have heard of some of these: predicate nominative, predicative adjective, direct object, indirect object, object of the preposition.

Predicables are the relations between the parts of speech, especially the relation between the subject and the parts of speech that make up the predicates. Take "Clark Kent became Superman." Here we have the nouns "Clark Kent" and "Superman," and the verb "became." These are the parts of speech, literally, the parts of the sentence.

But what about the relationships between the parts? Well, firstly, "Clark Kent" is related to the rest of the sentence as that which is being talked about, so, syntactically, it is called the subject. What about "Superman"? It's what's being predicated of "Clark Kent," but even more specifically, it is being predicated as what the subject *is*, what Clark Kent *is*, that is, it names him. So, we call this a subject *complement*, in this case, a *predicate nominative* (from the Latin *nomen*, which means "name.") There are other ways we could have talked about the subject without naming it: "Clark Kent is stopping the train." In this case, the predicate is stating what the subject is *doing*, and "train" is the noun that is receiving the doing. So, it is called the *direct object* of the doing.

The *syntax* of the sentence is the relationship that the words have to each other, including their function in the sentence.

You can see that these syntactical or relational labels don't make sense unless there is a relation of words, unlike the parts of speech which make sense on their own by themselves. Try to answer this question: What is the part of speech of "boat." Noun, you say. Right. But now answer this question. What is the *syntax* of "boat"? If you didn't have the sentence in which "boat" was included, you wouldn't be able to answer the question. You can only say that "boat" is a direct object if you look at what role it has in the sentence, where you can say that "boat" is a noun without needing a sentence at all.

All this is analogous to the relation of the categories to the predicables. The categories are like the parts of speech, and the predicables are like the syntax. You can only identify the predicables in relation to the subject of a proposition (the logical term for "sentence"), whereas you can identify the categories without a proposition.

OK, I'm going to illustrate this by giving you some examples of predicables before I define them. Here goes:

1) Sally is a rational animal.
2) Sally is an animal.
3) Sally is rational.
4) Sally is able to laugh.
5) Sally is in the room.

Ok, I bet you can name the categories. We've got a few substances, two different qualities, and one place. Predicables? Well, let's see if you can figure them out based only on your knowledge of the categories:

- Which of the predicates (what comes after the "is") describes the entire essence of Sally? We call this relation of subject and predicate *species*.
- Which of the predicates describes only part of Sally's essence? We call this relation of subject and predicate *genus*.
- Which of the predicates describe the essential quality of Sally, what makes her a human being and not just any animal? We call this relation of subject and predicate *specific difference*.
- Which of the predicates describe a non-essential quality of Sally that shows that she is human and not another kind of animal? We call this relation of subject and predicate *property*.
- Which of the predicates describes a non-essential aspect of Sally that does *not* show that she is human? We call this relation of subject and predicate *accident* .and not another kind of animal.

So, there are five predicables: genus, species, specific difference, and accident.

There are five predicables: genus, species, specific difference, and accident.

Can you see the connection with grammar now? The categories, the "say-ables about the be-ables," are the ten divisions of being, what every kind of being is in itself, and they are like the parts of speech when we analyze each word in a sentence. The predicables, the relations that a predicate can have to a subject, describe what every being is *in relation to another*, and they are thus like the syntactical terms when we analyze the relation of words in a sentence.

Categories

John is a man.

substance   substance

Parts of Speech

John is a man.

noun   verb   noun

Predicables

John is a man

subject   species

Syntax

John   is   a man

subject   linking verb   predicate nominative

There's also a nice connection between the predicables and extension. See if you can discover it through thinking about these examples:

- Man is an animal.
- Animal is a man.

Which one doesn't make sense? Why? Think about it for a few moments ...

Can you explain your answer in terms of extension? Try for a few minutes.

You may have figured out that the predicate *animal* in "Man is an animal" has a greater extension than the subject *man*. And that the predicate *man* in "Animal is a man" has a lesser extension. Yes, there are more animals than men. Can you create a rule about the predicables from your observations? Try for a few minutes.

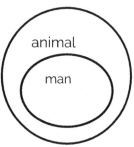

Here's the rule: A concept can only be predicated of another concept if it is greater in extension. In other words, the subject must have less extension than the predicate. The reason for this is that when we predicate something about some other thing, we are putting that some other thing into a category that includes it, and for the category to include it, it must be bigger than it.

Let's now talk a little about each predicable. For the first three predicables, species, genus, and difference, it will help us to look again at the Porphyrian tree (next page).

Can you find species, genus, and difference on the tree?

OK, let's take as our subject, "Sally." Let's predicate a genus of Sally. "Sally is a substance." So, according to our definition of genus, *substance* describes Sally's essence, but only partially. Surely Sally, being a human being, is not an accident like a color, but a substance, a being that exists in itself. She is essentially a substance, yes. But it doesn't tell us much about her essence, about what kind of being Sally really is. The extension of *substance* is too large, and the comprehension too small. This is why *substance*, in relation to Sally, is a genus, and a *remote* (distant) genus at that, since it's quite a distance up the tree from

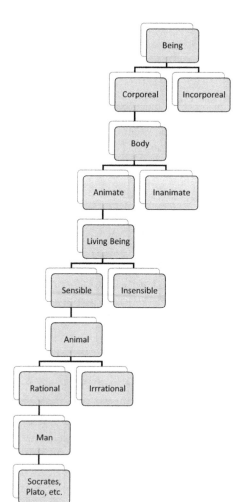

Sally's complete essence, a human being, which is her *species*. Now, the genus *animal* is also of Sally's essence, and partial, but it's closer to Sally's full essence, with a smaller extension and larger comprehension, so it's called a *proximate* or close genus. But how do we get to Sally's full essence? How do we lessen the extension of the proximate genus so that it includes only that group of beings of which Sally and others *essentially* like her are members, and no others? The answer is to "add" to the genus another predicable, namely, the one called *difference*.

Take a look at the top left branch of the tree. What happens when we include the generic difference *material* to the remote genus *substance*? Follow it down. We get the genus *body*. Let's see why. We can put it in the form of a sentence, in which *material* is added as an adjective to the noun (part of speech) and predicative nominative (syntax) *substance*.

Sally is a material substance.

But what is a material substance? A body! Notice how the addition of the difference *material* "shrinks" the extension of *substance* only to those substances that are bodies. The same thing happens when we add the specific difference *rational* to the proximate genus *animal*. We end up with only those animals that are rational, namely, human beings. "Animal" shrinks to "man" with the addition of "rational." And, thus, we arrive at the full essence of Sally, called her *species*.

Here's a puzzle. The concept *Man* contains all the concepts that make it up, such as substance and organism. That's because the concept *man* has a larger comprehension, and so, literally, comprehends them!

But *substance* comprehends *man*, in another way, does it not? Isn't substance more universal than man, in that there are more substances than there are men? We said before that we can't predicate something of another thing if it isn't more universal. That means when we say, "Man is a substance," substance must include and thus comprehend man. But how can *man* both include and be included by *substance*? Think about it for a few minutes.

The answer can be found in the relation of comprehension to extension. The comprehension of one concept is "bigger" than another concept when it has more conceptual parts, more notes. It's bigger *intellectually*, in that there's more conceptual stuff there, more thought material. Thus, *man* is bigger than *substance* because there's a lot more to think about when we consider a man than when we consider a substance. The more abstract and vague, that is, the further from particular and definite beings, the less conceptual content there is.

But the extension of one concept is bigger than another for the opposite reason. Extension is the amount of beings in the real world to which the concept refers, so a very abstract concept like *substance* refers to A LOT of beings in the real world! A less abstract concept like *man* does refer to a lot of beings, but not merely as many as *substance*. So, in one sense, *man* is bigger than substance, and, on the other, *substance* is bigger than *man*.

So, we have:

- **Genus**: the predicable that describes the partial essence of the subject: Sally is an animal.
- **Species**: the predicable that describes the full essence of the subject: Sally is a rational animal.
- **Difference**: the predicable that describes the defining quality of the genus of the subject (generic difference) or species of the subject (specific difference): Sally is material, living, sentient (generic difference). Sally is rational (specific difference).

We have two more predicables to talk about: property and accident.

- **Property**: the predicable that describes a quality that necessarily belongs only to the species of the subject but is not essential to it.
- **Accident:** the predicable that describes a quality that does not necessarily belong to the species of the subject.
- Sally is able to laugh.
- Sally is in the room.

Which one is a property and which is an accident?

Sally is a rational animal, and one of the indications of a rational being is that she can find something funny and laugh. She can, for example, see in her mind the incongruity between her expectation of what will happen, and what actually happens. Such incongruity sometimes makes us laugh. Now, even though being able to laugh is a feature of all rational beings and no non-rational beings, it is not an *essential* feature of rational beings. Instead, it is a quality that *derives* from the essential quality of rationality. So, "being able to laugh" is a property of rationality.

The fact that Sally laughs is because she is rational. The fact that she is in the room is not, for she could be in the room and not be a human being, like the plant next to her. And she could be human and not be the room, like she was 10 minutes ago when she was sitting outside. Thus, "in the room" is an accident.

Not all accidents are equally accidental. Compare "Sally is in the room" to "Sally is a mother." Both being in the room and being a mother are not essential to a human being, for many humans are neither in a room nor are mothers. But not only are humans not necessarily in a room, but also Sally herself can change from being in the room to not being in the room. The same is not true for the motherhood of Sally, if she is a mother. Let us say that she is a mother. Even though Sally could be human without being a mother, the fact that she is now a mother is not something she can change. This maternal relationship to a child is still accidental to being human, for not all humans are mothers, and it could have been the case that Sally did not become a mother, but now that she is a mother, it has become a quality of hers that is unchangeable, unlike being in the room. Can you think of other examples of accidents differing in the level of "accidentalness"?

Well, we're almost done with this book. Just one more chapter. There is just one more topic to cover in this course on material logic, and it just happens to be very important, like many things that come at the end of things. It is, in fact, the culmination of all that has gone before. We have studied words, grammar, the three acts of the intellect, the categories, form and matter, essence, concepts, comprehension and extension, and the predicables. All of these are different aspects of the first act of the intellect (even our study of the second and third acts shed much light on the nature of the first), and so are necessary in order to understand the goal of simple apprehension, which is not just to produce a concept in the mind, but to *define* it.

Definition is the perfection of simple apprehension, for it is in defining beings according to the predicables of genus and species that we come to know them most perfectly, most truly, which is, after all, the ultimate purpose of our minds, with logic one of the best tools.

Think for yourself...

Answer these in your own words:

1) What is a predicable?
2) Name and define the five predicables.
3) Come up with your own example for each of the five predicables, using a sentence for each example.
4) How do the predicables differ from the categories?
5) Explain how the predicables are like the syntax of a sentence, and the categories like the parts of speech.

Ponder this:

6) Do you think there might be some ethical, moral, or political issues that bear upon the predicables? Consider, for example, the issue of racism: the belief in the superiority or inferiority of one race to another, that one race is more or less human than another. How can the predicables, with some help from the categories, help with understanding this belief and even critiquing it? Think of another example of a moral or political issue that the predicables can help us think through and accurately about.

Lesson 10: *Definition: Simple Apprehension, Perfected*

With definition, we arrive at the outermost boundary of the first act of the intellect, and the entranceway to the second act. For, in simple apprehension, we not only encounter and then conceptualize the essence of some being, but also *understand* and *articulate* what we encounter and conceptualize. We need to formulate and express our concepts in order to better understand them. Definition helps us do this.

There are logical rules that must be followed in order to have a good definition, and we will look at these presently. But first, an important philosophical consideration, which brings us back to our discussion of truth in the first chapter. Definition involves more than logical rules. We can use logic to analyze given definitions of beings to see if the rules have been obeyed and to identify the kind of definition we are looking at. However, logic alone cannot verify whether or not the definition is the correct one, that is, if it describes actually *what* the essence of the being is. Why not?

Whether or not we have apprehended a being's essence, formed the right concept of it, and accurately described this concept in a definition is a question of whether we have discerned the *truth*, which is to say, whether we have actually contacted reality and described it as it is. Logic can give us rules to determine whether an argument is valid (3rd act of intellect). Logic can help us to see if our terms are clear and our concepts accurately categorized (1st act of intellect). And logic can show us how to categorize and relate various propositions together (2nd act). But what it can't do for us is determine whether our concepts and judgments are accurate to reality.

The truth of a proposed definition is judged by the human intellect in its second act. But whether we *know* if a definition is true depends on how well we are educated in the sciences, and how accurate these sciences are! Definitions about the material world are judged to be true in a systematic way, grounded by evidence, in the natural sciences (biology, chemistry, physics, etc.) and the philosophical sciences (the science of being, the science of knowledge, the science of right action — respectively, metaphysics, epistemology, ethics).

But even the sciences are not completely self-sufficient to determine the truth of things. The sciences are just the latest and hopefully most accurate expression of the inquiries of human beings over centuries. It is these cooperative inquiries into the nature of reality, full of struggle, failing, error, and revision, as well as the inquiries we do on our own based upon our own experience and thinking, that lead humans to truth. These inquiries never stop, for even the truths that have been discovered can always be better articulated, related more complexly to other truths, and more deeply understood. We can always gain a more fuller and deeper grasp of reality, and liberal and fine arts, such as literature, history, poetry, art, music, and dance, are just as powerful tools as science for grasping the mystery of reality.

When one's mind is in accordance with reality, we call this truth, and it is a relationship, a relationship of one's mind with the world. The sciences are true if they describe the world accurately, and we can only describe the world accurately if our minds are in the right relation to it. The arts and sciences, when they model and teach the truth, can help our minds to relate to the world rightly, but ultimately, we must accept the responsibility of searching for the truth ourselves, allowing reality to both determine the contents of our imaginations and minds, and measure them by its infallible standard.

In short, reality is the final authority. To know the truth, we must heed the wisdom that has come down to us, but we must also *seek this wisdom ourselves,* using the tools of logic, the sciences, literature, the arts, religion, and any other discipline, art, or field of human experience that can help us enter into and remain in a right relationship with reality.

Okay! It's time to get into the nitty-gritty of definition.

Recall our discussion of comprehension. We said that the comprehension of a concept is the description of its notes. Well, *definition* is the expression of the comprehension of a concept, and the best definition, the one that gets at a being's essence, does this using the predicables of *proximate genus* and *specific difference*. Take the essential definition of a human being as a "rational animal." *Animal* is the genus of a human being, and it contains within it all the notes that make it up, namely, substance, body, and organism. *Rational* is the specific difference of a human being, for it is what contracts the genus animal to only those animals that are rational, namely, human beings. So, "rational animal" expresses concisely and accurately the comprehension of *human being*.

If indeed it is the case that all human beings are, in their essence, rational animals, then with this definition we have successfully exercised the first act of the intellect. There are other real definitions of man using other predicables, such as, "a being that laughs" or "featherless bi-ped," and these are not false or unreal definitions, for they do distinguish men from other beings. But they are not as perfect as the definition by proximate genus and specific difference, because they do not get at the essence.

> **Definition** is the expression of the comprehension of a concept and the best definition does this using the predicables of *proximate genus* and *specific difference*.

The second act of the intellect begins where the first leaves off, taking the definition, "rational animal," and making a proposition out of it, namely, "Man is a rational animal," or, to put it in correct logical form, "All men are rational animals."

One example of something studied in the second act of the intellect is the relation of propositions to each other. Just to whet your appetite for more logic in the future, take a look at the diagram below. This is called the "Square of Opposition." In this version, we can make "S" equal to "man" and "P" equal to "rational." So we get four propositions and their various relations to each other:

(A) Every man is rational
(E) No man is rational
(I) Some men are rational,
(O) Some men are not rational.

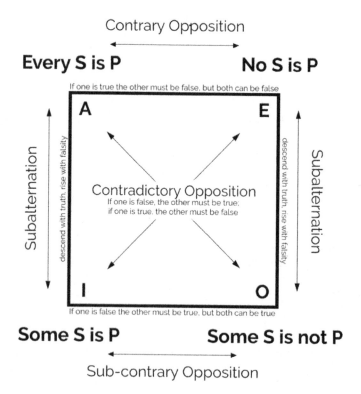

If A is true, what about E, I, and O? If we know that I is true, do we necessarily know that A is true? And there are many more questions! Have you ever come across a definition of a word that is a *correct* definition, but doesn't help you that much to figure out what the heck the thing is?

Consider:

Man: A human being.

Well that's fine if I already know what a human being is! But if you were talking to an alien from another planet who has never met a human being, and he asked what a man was, and you told him "a human being," it wouldn't help him much. Or how about:

Virtuous: That which possesses virtue.

Ok, but if I really want to know what virtue is, because I don't know, then this definition does not help me at all.

These are what are called *nominal* definitions, for they don't do much more than give you the definition of the *word,* as opposed to the real being to which the word refers.

Virtuous: That which possesses a good habit.

Now, this might seem like a nominal definition, for it feels just too simple, but actually, it's a *real* definition, one that describes the real being to which the word refers. And not only that, it's an essential definition! A virtue really is defined essentially as a good habit! This is how the classical philosophers defined it, and they knew what they were talking about when they talked about virtue, for it was a main preoccupation of the Ancient Greeks, and they pretty much discovered the reality of virtue and defined the concept. And it hasn't changed since their time.

Now, nominal definitions are not always helpful if we want to understand the meaning of *beings,* and not just other *words.* But there can also be *real* definitions that miss the mark. Consider these definitions of a human being:

Human being:	An animal that is not irrational
Human being:	An animal.
Human being:	The recapitulation of cosmic personality.
Human being:	A human-like being.
Human being:	The quintessence of dust.
Human being:	One of my friends.
Human being:	That substance endowed with a certain intellectual acumen, creativity, self-awareness, free will, ingenuity, capacity for love and hate, and inclination to good, but also transformative of both himself and his environment.

I think you can see that there is something not quite right about each of these definitions. The reason is that they all *disobey* — naughty definitions! — one of the six rules of logic. From Peter Kreeft[2], a master logician, we get the six rules for a logically acceptable definition:

1) A definition should be coextensive with the thing defined: neither too broad nor too narrow.
2) A definition should be clear, not obscure.
3) A definition should be literal, not metaphorical.
4) A definition should be brief, not long.
5) A definition should be positive, not negative, if possible. (Only negative realities call for negative definitions.)

---

[2] Kreeft, Peter, *Socratic Logic: First Edition* (South Bend, IN: Saint Augustine's Press, 2004), 124.

6) A definition should not be circular. (The term defined cannot appear in the definition.)

 Can you figure out what rule is broken by the six definitions of "human being" above?

So, we have discussed nominal definitions and bad definitions, but what about good ones? The best definition is one that tells us accurately and precisely what something is. But before we can *define* what something is, we need to *know* what it is. The way that we come to understand what something is is by observing it carefully, and by a successful operation of the first act of the intellect, we will have discerned its essence. We can then articulate the essence of the being by defining it in terms of its proximate (closest) genus and specific difference, thereby giving us the species, the substantial form, the "whatness" of the being (these are all different expressions for essence). This is the best kind of definition, for it not only differentiates the being from all other kinds of being, it also does so by zeroing in on the fundamental nature of the being, that is, what *causes* it to be what it is, which is the being's substantial form.

But there are other real definitions besides the essential one, and there are other causes for something to be, and to be what it is, besides its formal cause (its substantial form). In fact, sometimes we just don't know the essence of being, what causes it to be this kind of being and no other, and the best we can do is to describe the being in such a way as to set it apart from other beings that we think are essentially different from it.

Consider how we define non-human animals. What, precisely, is the essence of, say, a horse? Here's one dictionary's definition of it:

*a large solid-hoofed herbivorous ungulate mammal
(Equus caballus, family Equidae, the horse family)
domesticated since prehistoric times and used as a
beast of burden, a draft animal, or for riding.*

Certainly, this definition is accurate and good, neither too vague, too narrow, metaphorical, unclear, negative or circular — though it's a bit long! I can see the genus in there, *mammal*, but I'm not sure of the specific difference. Instead of giving a one-concept specific difference, such as *rational* in the definition of human being, it gives several properties and accidents. It also gives us a passion (in the categorical sense of something done to a being), telling us about its "having been domesticated." Finally, the definition gives us its purposes or functions for human beings.

Now consider the scientific definition of water: H_2O. Is this the substantial form of water, its essence, its whatness? Perhaps, but it's really just a description of the parts that make up water: two parts hydrogen and one part water. Is the essence of anything merely its parts? Perhaps on the elemental level this is the case, but what about at more complex levels. Is a human being well defined by giving the chemical makeup of the human body?

*Human being: A unique proportion of 99% Oxygen,
Carbon, Hydrogen, Nitrogen, Calcium, and Phos-
phorus, and 1% several other chemicals.*

Really?

But perhaps water also is not best defined by the matter that makes it up. We could define water by, say, its unique earthly purpose — "the universal solvent" — or we could define it more metaphorically, but perhaps more accurately, as "the elixir of life." The point I am trying to make here is that the ideal definition, the one that gives us the species of something through proximate genus and specific difference, is not always possible, and sometimes we can get at the real nature of a being by looking at its properties, function, and material components.

The Four Causes

Consider this definition of a chair:

> *A chair is a piece of furniture, usually made from wood or plastic, crafted by human beings for sitting.*

The proximate genus is "furniture" (a remote genus would be "artificial object"), but how should we categorize the other descriptors? Well, they are certainly properties of chairs, but "made from wood or plastic" and "made by human beings" are generic properties, properties of the proximate genus of chair, which is "furniture." This is because other things in the world are made of wood or plastic, and human beings make things other than furniture. "For sitting" is certainly a specific property of a chair, for no other kind of furniture is peculiarly for sitting as a chair (a stool, for example, is a specific kind of chair). So, here we have a definition made of genus and several properties, some generic, one specific.

But we can also look at this definition from another angle. What are the *causes* of a chair? Now, the first thing you think of, I bet, as the cause of a chair is a human being, in this case, a chairmaker (or if made in a factory by robots, a robot). But there are other causes too. Could a chair exist without wood or plastic or metal or some material? The chairmaker needs materials to work on. OK, do we have all the causes now? Not yet! The chairmaker is only able to make a chair because there is a blueprint, so to speak, for a chair, even if just in the chairmaker's mind. A chair has an organized structure, a form, and the chairmaker must consider in his mind this form as he crafts the chair. In short, there would be no chair without the "whatness" of a chair, "chairness" if you will. OK, I think we must be done now. But wait, there's more! In our definition above we have "for sitting." This doesn't seem like a cause of chairs, but think about it a little. "For sitting" is the purpose of chairs, and without a purpose, would chairs ever have been made? The cause of horses existing in the human world of commerce and transportation is because of their purposes, carrying people and bearing burdens. Of course, biologically, these purposes did not create horses. But they did cause horses to become domesticated animals.

So, we have four causes of beings, causes that can be used to define beings. The four causes not only tell us the what and the how, but the also the why. We don't fully know *what* something is unless we know *why* it is, as Aristotle wrote: "We do not have knowledge of a thing until we have grasped its why, that is to say, its cause."

Material Cause: What something is made of. What are its parts?
Formal Cause: What something is, its essence. What is it?
Efficient Cause: What or who brought the being into existence?
Final Cause: The purpose or function of the being. What's it *for*?

Notice that the first two causes are *internal* to the being, while the last two are *external*. Modern science tends to focus on the material and efficient causes, citing the efficient cause(s) as the sole explanation for why the being exists, and citing the material cause to explain why it behaves the way it does, as well as what it is. Classical philosophy included these two causes but focused more on the formal and final causes for explaining both the what and the why of beings.

It is easy to see that human artifacts, like tables and computers and bridges, have all four causes, but it's not so clear that organisms have all of them. As we discussed, it's hard to define the formal or final cause of a horse or water, though it does seem that they do have some sort of substantial form that makes them what they are and not something else. It's also not clear that we can reduce the form just to the matter, the parts of the horse or the elements in water. And we can see a final cause in horses if we relate them to human use, but what is a horse's purpose outside of human purposes? Why exactly do horses exist in themselves?

What about human beings? We know what human bodies are made of, but are just our bodies? What about consciousness and self-awareness and thinking? Can matter think and know itself? Aristotle thought that all organism had souls — even plants! — and that the soul was the "form of the body." What he meant by a soul was that which explains the essence of the organism, why it has life, and why it has the kind of body it does. Why do *these* sorts of beings interact with the environment in an active way, taking in nutrients, growing, and reproducing, with some even sensing and emoting? And why do *those* sorts of beings don't? For Aristotle, the answer is the presence of a soul, the principle of life. Humans can also think, and this meant that their soul was especially separate from matter, for as we have discussed, concepts seem to be immaterial things that exist in an immaterial mind.

The efficient cause of plants and animals are their "parent" plants and animals, and, more generally, nature — nature being an interconnected system of causes that gives and preserves life. People who believe in a divine source of life believe that the ultimate efficient cause for all things is God, with nature only an instrument that the divine created to bring about its purposes. Those who do not believe in a divine source might cite the process of evolution as an efficient cause and a sufficient explanation for life.

What about the final cause of animals, humans, and the whole universe? The first philosophical question, the one that underlies all others, is: Why is there something rather than nothing? Depending on our answer, we will define the beings in the universe and the universe itself in a way that correlates with it.

Here below is a great chart of definitions to study. You can spend hours on it! Out of the brilliant mind of Peter Kreeft:

DEFINITION[3]

KIND OF DEFINITION	OF 'MAN'	OF 'TRIANGLE'	OF 'DEMOCRACY'
too broad	two-legged animal	plane figure	form of government
too narrow	male rational animal	enclosed plane figure with three equal sides	government by direct popular rule
obscure	an ontological synthesis of molecular and self-referential intentionality	the two-dimensional figural foundation for geodesic domes	participatory or semi-participatory plebiscitarianism
metaphoric al	a ghost in a machine	the geometrical image of the Holy Trinity	a bunch of blind bats discussing the definition of daylight
too long	the most paradoxical and multi-dimensional creature in nature,	a two-dimensional geometric figure composed of no more	that form of government whose essential features include popular

---

[3] Kreeft, Peter, *Socratic Logic: First Edition* (South Bend, IN: Saint Augustine's Press, 2004), 127-129.

	exhibiting both visually detectable physical attributes and that form of consciousness which can become progressively more aware of a plurality of propositional truths by reasoning	and no less than three finite straight lines all of whose end points touch those of another, thereby enclosing a finite space	recall of elected officials, referenda on selected issues, majority rule, and legal equality of essential rights for all citizens
negative	neither ape nor angel	neither a one-dimensional line nor a three-dimensional solid, and neither a square nor a circle	"the most imperfect form of government ever invented except all the other ones" (Winston Churchill)
circular	the creature with human attributes	the shape of any triangular object	government by democratic process
nominal	The species called "*homo sapiens*"	English word for the following figure: Δ	English word for *archē* and *dēmos*

essential	rational animal	three-sided enclosed plane figure	government by popular sovereignty
by property	the animal that speaks	enclosed plane figure with 180° in its three interior angles	government in which laws are changed by popular consent
by accidents	the animal with two legs and no feathers	favorite geometrical figure of the late medieval mystics	form of government most prevalent in 20th-century Europe
by efficient cause	creature whose soul is directly created by God	enclosed plane figure generated by the meeting of three straight lines	form of government created by the American "Founding Fathers"
by final cause	the creature who seeks Truth, Goodness, and Beauty as ends	geometrical figure providentiall y designed to image the Trinity in two dimensions	government designed for the most participation for the most people
by material cause	the creature composed of an animal	the two-dimensional figure that contains a finite space,	government composed of citizens

| body and a rational soul | three straight lines, and three angles | enfranchised to vote |

Material Logic, the study of the first act of the intellect, can help us define the beings we encounter with clarity and distinctness. Formal logic, the study of the second and third acts of the intellect, can help us make rationally defensible claims about the world. But to answer the why questions we all wonder about, we need the help of all the liberal arts and sciences, as well as guidance from the wise, and a heart that loves truth and has the courage to seek it.

Well, we've come to the end of this chapter on definition, and the end of our book! Thank you for coming on this journey with me into words, concepts, and reality. Remember: If you correct your mind — and open your heart — the rest will fall into place!

Think for yourself...

Answer these in your own words:

1) Say what rule is being broken in each of these definitions, and explain your answer:
   - Human being: An animal that is not irrational
   - Human being: An animal.
   - Human being: The recapitulation of cosmic personality.
   - Human being: A human-like being.
   - Human being: The quintessence of dust.

- Human being: One of my friends.
- Human being: That substance endowed with a certain intellectual acumen, creativity, self-awareness, free will, ingenuity, capacity for love and hate, and inclination to good, but also transformative of both himself and his environment.

2) Explain why logic alone can't enable us to discover and know truth.
3) Describe the four causes in your own words.
4) Give each of the four causes for: a chair, a human being, the statue of David, thunder, the universe, the concept "horse," the science of logic (multiple answers are possible!).

Ponder this:

5) What was the most interesting topic of logic for you? Why? How has your thinking been "corrected" by studying logic? Have you been helped to come closer to reality? How? How do you think you can apply what you have learned about logic in your life?

Made in the USA
Las Vegas, NV
16 June 2022

50281445R00059